FINE WINES

THE BEST VINTAGES OF THE 20TH CENTURY

© 2000 Assouline Publishing

601 West 26th Street
18th floor
New York, NY 10001, USA

www.assouline.com

English translation: Josephine Bacon

Printed in Italy

ISBN: 2 84323 207 4 (US edition) / 284323 237 6 (UK)

MICHEL DOVAZ

FINE WINES

THE BEST VINTAGES OF THE 20TH CENTURY

ASSOULINE

INTRODUCTION

Of all the books on my favorite subject that have passed through
my hands in recent years, I can honestly say that few have held
for me such fascination as Michel Dovaz's *Fine Wines*.
The reason is easy to see but rather more complicated to explain.
Indeed, like a fine wine, it speaks for itself. Also, like a fine wine,
it not only appeals immediately to the senses but, the more one
sips and tastes, the more is revealed.
What I am trying to say is that *Fine Wines* works on several levels.
First, one notices the illustrations which are a feast for the eye:
a veritable kaleidoscope of color which manages
to reflect the wide ranging scenes, varying from "close ups" to
panoramic views, interspersed cunningly with double page spreads
in black and white which encapsulate and evoke each period.
But, however attractive the presentation, the meat of the book
is the written word. Michel Dovaz is in a league of his own.
I cannot think of any English writer, and there are many, who has
the same approach to wine. If I use the term "intellectual", it
might sound dry, perhaps even off putting. But, the truth of the
matter is that Dovaz displays in all his work an original mind.
There is nothing second hand about his opinions. He brings a
freshness of approach and a rare sensitivity to what many of us
wine lovers take for granted.
In the first part of the book, he takes us through the essentials:
what exactly is needed to produce fine wines? The constant
factors, which nevertheless vary from country to country, district
to district : soil, subsoil, drainage—so mundane yet so crucial.

The factors beyond man's control, the climate and its variables, which have such an effect on quality; and those which are at the disposition of the producer, from grape varieties and clones to vine husbandry, wine making, and that French term "élevage" which, like "terroir," has no precise equivalent.

To be frank, once most of us have mastered, or at least are aware of the basics, we tend to take them for granted. But I frequently remind myself that it is so easy for us to select, to buy, to taste, to criticize, to drink—and so difficult, so risky, so expensive to produce the wines which provide us with such a wealth of interest and enjoyment.

In the second and necessarily extensive part of the book, indeed the core of the work, the century of wines is handled in a direct yet ingenious way. Dovaz introduces each period by reminding us of significant events and personalities; setting the scene, historically and evocatively. Then—for this is his tour de force—picking out the greatest vintages and illustrating them with the most perfect examples of wine produced in each of these years. Moreover, and I have not seen it done before, to encapsulate the particular features and qualities of each representative wine. As this happens to be my particular area of expertise, such as it is, I followed the progress of these vignettes (rather an appropriate term to sum up a description of vine, wine and vintage) with particular attention and growing excitement. What vintages, what wines had Dovaz selected; and had he missed any out? Not really. Of course, one could argue that perhaps another vintage, another wine could, should, have been included. In fact, all the truly great examples are in the text. Yet, to be fair, Dovaz lists the "also rans" under "other great vintages" (and wines) towards the end of the book.

I am entranced, and hope the reader will be, by the wealth of factual, instructive, vivid, tantalizing descriptions and evocative pictures. Well done Dovaz and Assouline!

Michael Broadbent
Christie's, London

Part I
The Very Great Wines

*"Can you imagine, my whole fortune depends
on three hours of sunshine."*

MICHEL DE MONTESQUIEU
(in a letter to Madame Dupré de Saint-Maur,
wife of the Comptroller of Finance)

Part I
The Very Great Wines

Preface

It must be admitted that as we move into a new millennium, there is a great temptation to take stock, and decide what were the greatest films the best automobiles, the most famous people, and so on, of the last century.

The idea of a book on the subject of the greatest wines of the century thus came naturally to my publisher, Prosper Assouline, who is a great wine buff.

Covering a century of œnological creation could truly be termed "mission impossible," unless the arbitrary nature of a challenge such as this which I have agreed to accept is recognized as such and allowances are made.

In reality, producing a shortlist of the great wines of the century means compiling a list of the vintage years, because as far as vineyards are concerned, it is the year in which the wine was produced, i.e. the vintage, which is the determining factor.

This book is not an encyclopedia but an anthology. Or, more precisely, a garland of the greatest vintages of the century, in which each flower is the wine or wines which are the best representative of their kind.

By no means all the great wines are included in these pages, but each of those chosen symbolizes what is best and most distinctive in a great vintage from a particular region.

Can the twentieth century be considered a "good century"? Has it produced its share of good years? Only one element of comparison can be used in reply to this question—the nineteenth century.

While assessments of quality can only be approximations, it is worth

Climat de la Romanée

Rapport d'estimation
du Domaine de la
Romanée situé à Vosne
Canton de Nuits.

Curey, le 27 Messidor
an 2.^e

N.º 124.

aff. 147.

Henry Renaudot

demeurant à Gilly et Joseph Durand demeurant
à Nuits, Experts nommés par Arrêté du Directoire
du District de Dijon, du 23 Prairial dernier, pour procéder
aux Visite et estimation des Vignes et Bâtiments composant
le Domaine appellé la Romanée Conty. De faire un
rapport très détaillé sur la propriété dont il s'agit, sur son
produit ancien et actuel, et enfin sur tout ce qui peut intéresser
les acquereurs, touchant l'historique de ce fameux Vignoble.

Certifions, qu'après avoir prêté le Serment requis par devant
le Juge de Paix de la Commune dudit Nuits, le onze Messidor
présent mois, Nous nous sommes le même jour, transporté
à la Commune de Vosne; et nous étant addressé au Citoïen
Jean Mougeard Agent national dudit Vosne, dont le père
a cultivé pendant quarente huit ans, la Vigne dont est question,
Nous l'avons invité de nous accompagner dans nos operations
Et de nous procurer, ainsi que Denis Mougeard son frère, les
renseignements qui nous seront nécessaires, Ce à quoi lui et
l'autre s'étant prêté, Nous nous sommes transporté sur la
Pièce de Vigne appellée la Romanée Conty, que nous avons
parcourue et visité attentivement dans toute son étendüe, et
ensuite dans les Bâtiments et dépendances d'iceux faisant
partie du même Domaine, lesquels nous avons également parcouru
et visité dans toutes leurs parties, et Nous avons vu et
reconnu ce qui suit, Savoir.

La Romanée.

Est une pièce de Vigne, Célèbre par la qualité exquise du

noting two coincidences: in the course of both centuries, the thirties were relatively unproductive, with the possible exception of the 1834 and 1937 vintages. The years '88, '89 and '90, on the other hand, were excellent in the nineteenth and twentieth centuries. In fact, Nature has proved to be extremely fair and one can count on a great year approximately once every ten years as well as three better-than-average years (including "the" great year). There may be dramatic changes of climate ahead in the new century, resulting from the greenhouse effect. This may cause changes in the Gulfstream and other ocean currents due to the reduction in the polar ice cap, but an examination of the past two centuries reveals considerable stability in the climate and thus the consequences for the vineyard.

It is also interesting to note that the vicissitudes of the economy have done nothing to affect the market in the highest quality wines. Production remains limited, demand is small in volume but consistent and quite independent of economic crises because it emanates from a moneyed clientele.

In fact, the great wines of the great vintages are "loners." They remain impervious, independent, far from the madding crowd.

They are beacons illuminating a landscape which may be tranquil or turbulent, flat or rugged, busy or featureless—whatever their surroundings, they remain superbly indifferent to them.

This book will at least reveal who and what they are—even if it is not possible to sample them!

It tells the story of a century of great vintages.

Preceding page: first page of a valuation report
on the Romanée-Conti Estate.
Facing page: the Jadot cellars, Jacobin convent, Beaune.

Introduction

Three levels of quality are normally used as yardsticks to assess whether a wine is excellent, good, or average, but excellence is all that concerns us here.

Below:
wine-tasting in a
cellar.

Excellence is not a uniform characteristic, but the best of the excellent becomes the outstanding, and the outstanding is all that we are concerned with in this book.

Facing page:
tasting a
Vosne-Romanée.

Despite all this, in a world in which everything is measured and assessed, is it possible to speak of evaluation methods in relation to wines as rare as those which are about to be discussed? Not really. The birth of a great wine is heralded by rumor. The rumor is confirmed by its persistence, and tastings indicate whether or not it is well-founded. The whole problem of assessing an outstanding wine lies not in its nature, which, when all is said and done, differs little from that of a good wine, but in a set of factors that are as essential as they are infinitessimal, even indescribable. Œnologists are fully aware of the measurable constituents of wine, its percentage of alcohol, level of acidity, tannin content, residual sugars, and the volatile acidity that should not be exceeded, as well as

Sauternes

the acceptable sulfur level (combined and free), and so on. They can thus determine, without even tasting the wine, whether it is "of saleable quality" or whether it is unfit for human consumption. An appreciation of the quality of a wine lies elsewhere. Only a tasting can make things clear by combining the tactile impressions, an assessment of the aroma and "length in the mouth." Tasting alone reveals the balance and harmony resulting from several hundreds of items of information which combine, juxtapose, compensate, counteract, or complement each other in the various receptors of the olfactory organ.

When it is realized that the human nose can normally distinguish between four hundred thousand odors, which ought to be imperceptible (since they are carried in a millionth of a milligram per liter of air), it can be seen that words are quite inadequate to describe a wine, whether great or unexceptional, and justify, or merely explain, why one wine is exceptional and another is not. A very great wine must fulfill two conditions. It must have absolute balance and a perfect aromatic harmony. A number of essays on wine have defined balance by using spatial representations indicating a focal point in order to symbolize the golden mean between acidity, mellowness, and astringency. Harmony, on the other hand, or if you prefer, aromatic balance, cannot be described in words; concepts of strength, richness, purity, finesse, and aromatic complexity have to be taken into account.

A wine that is average in quality may be balanced and may even tend to possess a simple harmony. The harmony will be judged as being simple due to its limited number of aromatic components, which may not be powerful enough, pure enough, or perhaps complex enough.

A very great wine, on the other hand, is conspicuous by its perfect balance which is aromatically harmonious, pure, powerful, and above all, complex. It is rare for any great wine not to be "long in the mouth."

Experience shows that the evidence for aromatic complexity is the appearance of what are called tertiary aromas or aromas of aging. A very great wine must therefore be a wine which possesses great

The nose.

longevity. Various factors may contribute to the longevity of a wine. These include the grape variety, age of the vine, vinification and, above all, the territory on which it grows, the term "territory" embracing both soil conditions and climate.

The Land, a Constant

Where viticulture is concerned, the concept of land is fairly vague. Two parameters must be taken into account, apart from that of the climate— human intervention and the soil.

Human Intervention

Without this, the land would never reveal itself. Humans must discover the most suitable vine stock for the soil type, who must improve the land through drainage or by tilling the soil. In the countries of Europe which have a long wine-making tradition (those which produce the great vintages), the adaptation between grape variety and land is definitive, at least as long as the current organoleptic prototypes persist. On the other, the countries that are termed "new producers" may well experience certain changes.

Vineyard
on the early slopes
of Bordeaux.

It should be noted however, that human intervention is becoming ever more restricted now that propagation and growing techniques are becoming uniform through teaching.

The Soil

The soil type is fundamental. It is not a question of whether or not a grape vine will grow in a particular soil but of whether it is capable of producing grapes of high quality. In this respect, the absence of water retention is an essential condition. As early as 1857, the ampelographer, Victor Rendu, wrote: "The vine adapts to any kind of terrain as long as water does not stagnate on it."

It is thus recognized that pure clay, with its very fine granulometry is unsuitable for viticulture.

The whole subject becomes more complicated when one realizes that in transverse section, the soil looks like a slice of flaky pastry whose various layers are different in type and thickness.

The water table, its distance from the surface, and the source of its water supply, constitute another fundamental element that must be taken into account.

The filtering capability of the soil is a vital factor, but it must also be able to restore water — generally by capillary migration—is also very important, especially during dry summers. The orientation of the slopes, their gradient and environment also play an important part. Over and above the physical aspect of the soil, there is its chemical composition. Here, several thousand factors are involved, all of which play their own part in feeding the vine.

Even though the principal agents for improving the vitality of a vine stock are well-known, it is infinitely harder to determine the chemistry which differentiates a Château Lafite from a Château Mouton Rothschild. The combination of these determining factors at their best is the basis for the creation of great wines, but the plethora of complex data is what makes it so hard to analyze them.

The Climate, a Variable

On the other hand, we are better equipped to perform climatic analysis.

Meteorological stations regularly report the air temperature, percentage of humidity, rains (in inches or millimeters per day), etc.

This data, however summary, recorded over the annual growing period, is sufficient to indicate the quality of a vintage.

The Vintages

Bernard Ginestet conducted research in the Bordeaux district in the 1970s concerning the consequences of climatic variables. It is summarized here in the form of a graphic, but was the result of a long and arduous study, which took five factors into account:

- maximum temperature,
- minimum temperature,
- number of hours of sunshine,
- number of hours of rain,
- depth of precipitation.

The formula he obtained appears to be fairly balanced because about half of the wines are above average, the other half below.

A very great vintage involves other factors, however, including the need for temperatures above 30°C (86°F). It is therefore important to know the number of days or hours on which the temperature exceeded 30°C (86°F) and the amount and distribution of sunshine as the grapes ripened. In this respect, Émile Peynaud notes that the quality of the grape harvest is mainly conditional upon the amount of sunshine in the months of August and September, but he adds, "it can be said that the weather in the last week counts for double."

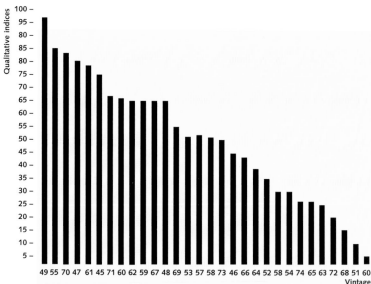

Facing:
Châteauneuf-du-Pape vine stock.

Heat and dryness are almost always favorable conditions, unless a severe drought impedes growth, starving the grape of sugar, or if the sun broils it to a frazzle. On the other hand, although there are beneficial rains (the famous storm of August 15), others are catastrophic. If it rains during a hot spell on ripe grapes, they will rot immediately, and if grapes have to be harvested in the rain, this will inevitably result in loss of quality.

These generalizations in relation to climate and how it affects the vintage ought also to take account of two special cases, namely the influence of a microclimate, which requires the set of data to be collected in the field and not at a weather station, which may well be located several dozen miles from the vineyard, and the special position of the vineyard in relation to the others that enjoy the same appellation.

Finally, a very great vintage is the result of a particular configuration of the bunch of grapes. It is imperative that the individual grapes be small and that they have a thick skin, especially in the case of red wines. This is easily understood if one takes account of the relationship between the volume of liquid (the volume of must) and the surface of the skin. For a given volume, the larger the surface of the skin, the more concentrated the extraction, since all the elements which constitute the wine, with the exception of the sugar, are concentrated in the skin of the grape. There is a dual advantage in the grape having a thick skin. This makes it resistant to attacks from disease and insects and increases the quantity of extractable elements.

Below: bunch of Pinot Noir grapes.

Facing page: vines in the rain.

Climate and Land

Clos de Vougeot, a huge, hilly enclosed vineyard, does not react uniformly to climatic variations. In the course of an average year, the upper and central areas of the enclosure produce the best wines, and the lower-lying plots receive all the runoff (especially as the Route Nationale 74, runs above and beside the land on an embankment which certainly never existed in the twelfth century when the

Cistercian monks created their vineyard). On the other hand, in years of serious drought—1976, for example—the lower-lying plots were the best. The quality of a territory, in the geological sense of the term, has nothing absolute about it, since each parcel reacts differently to the vagaries of the climate depending on its own geological features, as well as its altitude, gradient, and the surrounding environment (hilltop, valley bottom, etc.). Under these conditions, the ideal vineyard would be one planted on a territory capable of adapting to all the possible weather conditions without losing its quality, and giving of its best under all circumstances. Does such a territory exist? No statistical survey of the plasticity coefficient (adaptability to the climate) of plots of land or estates has ever been produced. Yet everyone knows of or has heard of a château or an estate which is famous for being able to produce minor vintages on a regular basis.

Château Latour in the Bordeaux district has such a reputation. An examination of the Château Latour territory reveals the secret of its plasticity. The ground is particularly poor and with maximum filtration capacity (porosity) in its first 80 centimeters (this is called the topsoil), while the subsoil below it consists of clay loam which contributes richness and humidity.

These various observations lead one to wonder whether there is such a thing as a vineyard grown on a soil that has no plasticity whatsoever and which only rarely produces an exceptional wine, for example every ten years or every twenty years.

Theoretically, there is nothing to stop this happening, although the production of a great wine assumes great investments and perfect mastery of the technique. Hence the conclusion, which might be judged an exaggeration, of the wine expert Roger Dion, who wrote in 1959: "The quality of a wine is not so much the expression of a natural milieu, but is considered as the expression of a social milieu."

There is a region of France in which investment, skill, technical prowess and the "social milieu"—to borrow Roger Dion's expression—are all at their peak. It is in that part of Champagne which

Geological cross-section of soil in the Bordeaux district.

produces red wines. In about one year in ten, certain Bouzy
Rouges, or an Ay Rouge (the Côte aux Enfants de Bollinger, for
example), manage to haul themselves up to the dizzying heights of
an outstanding wine. (Two other factors come into play here which
will be discussed later, namely archetypes and volumes of
production.)

Finally, as soon as it is admitted that great wines are born at the limit of
the growing range of a vine variety, the question must be asked as to
whether this limit can be pushed back when exceptional climatic
conditions prevail (this question really only applies to vines used to make
white wines.) It can well be imagined that many vineyards have been
abandoned because they could only produce an outstanding wine on
rare occasions. There are several examples in French history. For
instance, the hill of Coucy, in Picardy, topped by an imposing ruined
castle, might be considered an ideal place to plant a vine, and this is a

Late 19th century British advertisement for the House of Bollinger.

perfectly reasonable assumption because in the late Middle Ages, Coucy wine had an extremely high reputation. But Coucy lies too far to the north, and the Fromental variety (*alias* Pinot Gris) only achieved full ripeness on rare occasions. Yet when it managed to do so, all of the finesse of the north was brought to bear in a balanced acidity and sufficient percentage of alcohol to produce a white wine of very great lineage. Its unreliability proved fatal, however.

This the vineyard of Coucy, long gone alas, belongs to the category of "fantom vintages" which would otherwise have found their place in this book, alongside the greatest wines.

Climate and Vines

Facing page: menu by Alain Chapel, 1979 (Archives of the Château de Fesles).

The vegetative cycle is the succession of stages in the life of a vine between two periods of *dormancy*.

In temperate countries, in the winter, the vine sleeps. Vines prefer cold winters, since the cold destroys many of their parasites. Winters that are

À l'apéritif :

Petite friture de goujons du lac d'Annecy, persil & fanes de céleris frits,
Pieds de cheval, pleine mer ooooo & bouquet breton,

Gelée de pigeonneaux, trois sot l'y laisse & jeunes légumes,

Côteaux des sables de Vendée, en chaud-froid d'estragon,
toute petite salade de baraquets.

Xérès, très vieux Porto 1937
magnum Cristal Rœderer 1973
Bonnezeaux 1947 - Château de Fesle
Pêches blanches

Petit feuilleté de grenouilles de pays, d'écrevisses "pattes rouges"
& mousserons des prés, au cerfeuil

Poularde de Bresse, dans sa gelée, en terrine
petite salade de cèpes & premières truffes

Bassine de langoustes rouges bretonnes à la nage au meursault

Salade de roquette, reine des glaces, feuilles de chêne & éclergeons,
de canette de barbarie à l'huile de noix & aux chapons

Quelques fromages fermiers

Glace crème vanille & sorbet de pêches de vigne,
fruits rouges de Thurins
Glace crème pistaches & poires Williams au beurre,
tartes aux pralines
Aveline anniversaire & confiture d'oranges amères
Mignardises, candis & chocolats
Les cafés

too cold, however, can do a lot of damage. If brief spells of −20°C (4°F) do little harm, if they are prolonged, the vine stock will freeze and die. In the spring, the soil temperature grows warmer. When it reaches 10–11°C (50-52°F), the vegetative cycle is triggered. The sap rises, buds appear and burst forth, and *budding* begins. Twigs and branches cannot begin to develop until the air temperature is higher than 10°C (50°F). Then there are several important stages which involve the formation of the bunches of grapes.

Inflorescences lead to *flowering,* in early June.

The temperature must be at least 17°C (63°F).

If flowering is unsuccessful because the weather is too cold, the flower will not open, pollination is impossible, the grape does not form, and there is *wilt.* Heavy rain can do similar damage.

After fertilization, the grapes are formed, it is the start of *fruiting.* From late July, *maturing* begins and is indicated by a change in the color of the grapes: white grapes become translucent, and black grapes begin to darken.

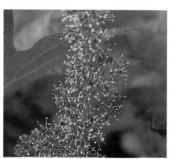

Simultaneously, the vine stops growing. During this phase, the plant begins to store the nutrients it will need when it starts its growing season again in the spring.

French grapes attain full ripeness in September. Meanwhile, the leaves turn yellow and begin to fall. The *shedding* is the last phase before dormancy.

So throughout the cycle, it can be seen that climatic conditions are decisive and are responsible for the volume and quality of the harvest.

Note however:

• The relationship between quantity and quality is not as simple as one has been led to believe. Very small harvests have sometimes produced poor quality wines (in Bordeaux, examples are 1957 and 1969).

Large harvests, on the other hand, can achieve high

quality (as they did in Bordeaux in 1982 and 1990). On the other hand, the huge harvest of 1973 was spoiled by defects and dilution. And again, the very small harvests of 1945 and 1961 produced legendary wines.

• It is always difficult to compare a wine that *exists* with a wine that *might have been*. In other words, it cannot be claimed that 1982 or 1990 would have been better years if the yield per acre or per hectare had been smaller. Many experts nevertheless take this view, and the use of reverse osmosis, a vinification technique which is designed to reduce the yield per hectare after the event, seems to prove them right.

• Nature offers ample evidence of her fertile imagination: no two years are ever alike.

Even the exceptional vintages, the ones which interest us here, were the result of an extraordinary diversity of climatic conditions.

There are several types of vintages:

Quantitatively: small crops, average crops, and heavy crops.

Qualitatively: poor, average, and excellent vintages.

Where soil type and grape variety do not vary, it is solely the weather conditions that are responsible for these variations in the result.

It should thus be no surprise to learn that average vintages are the result of average or normal weather conditions.

Finally, here are a few examples of circumstances that can arise:

• Small harvest imply frost, wilting, and sometimes drought.

• Abundant harvests are the result of the right weather conditions, rain coming at just the right time, warmth and large grapes.

• Poor vintages are a sign that the grapes did not ripen sufficiently, as a result of lack of sunshine, rot, or, much more rarely, stunted growth due to drought. It often rains during the harvesting season.

• The great vintages are the result of an exceptional amount of sunshine, heatwaves, a sprinkling of summer rain (on August 15) and harvesting being possible in dry weather. Under these conditions, the grapes themselves are generally very small.

Left and right: the fall and harvesting
as it used to be at Château Latour.
Following pages: falling leaves at Clos d'Estournel.

Outstanding Vintages

When the conditions for the birth of outstanding vintages are studied, it will be seen that Nature works on the basis of two possible scenarios. The first is obvious and logical, perhaps even a cliché, namely, that the weather must be just right from Spring through Fall. The years 1929, 1959, 1982 and 1990 belong to this category.

The second condition, more unexpected although recurring, has proved to be particularly effective. The principle is simple. It consists in a draconian reduction of the yield per hectare, resulting in a grape of exceptional maturity. In general, an early spring favors swift opening of the buds. Then a sharp frost will dampen off the buds, sparing only a very few. Occasionally, the initial damage is repeated, making flowering difficult and causing more buds to wither and die. From June through late September, the weather needs to be very dry and very hot, though a brief downpour will prevent the plant from drying out too much. That is how some of the great vintages were born, especially those of 1921, 1945, and 1961.

The great vintages that will be discussed in the second part of this book have become milestones of the twentieth century. Their yields provide an opportunity to analyze their achievements and attempt to understand what went into the creation of an exceptional wine. Anyone tempted to single out the "best" vintage of the century (1921?) and the "worst" (1910?) should be conscious of the subjectivity of individual judgement. As will be shown later, the combination of new developments in technique and natural factors make it extremely difficult, if not

Facing page :
exceptional
vintages
on sale at
Christie's.

Auction at the
Hôtel Drouot,
Paris.

impossible, to compare great wines. It is more a question of knowing
whether such comparisons involve the quality of the wines of a
particular vintage or whether it is an attempt to evaluate nature's bounty
in a particular year. Have vine-growers and wine-makers always been
able to get the best out of Nature, starting in 1900? To reply in the
affirmative would be to deny that any new developments had taken
place, that there had been any progress. It would be the equivalent of
believing that grapes and wines had never been improved through new

vinification methods, changes in planting techniques, grape varieties, and so on, and to claim that the tastes of teh consumer have not altered

Entrance to the winestore at Château Latour early 19th century (above).
Omega grafting at Romanée-Conti (center).
Spraying the vines in Burgundy (below).

one iota. This is not the appropriate place to determine which factor influences which, production or taste. On the other hand, the developments which have affected the vineyards are worthy of examination. What happened in the twentieth century that had such repercussions on the organoleptic qualities of wine? Despite the fact that the great wines have changed far less than the ordinary wines, there are nevertheless a few important moments and milestones to be recorded. These include:

* the replacement of the horse by the tractor;

* changes in spraying (systemic and combination chemicals to protect the plant from the inside, as opposed to superficial protection) and the use and abuse of chemical sprays;

* the invention of chemical weed-killers, which eliminate the need to till the soil; in the best vineyards, partial tilling has been reintroduced, leaving grass and some weeds to grow again;

* the improved adaptation of root-stocks to various soils, a change from root-stocks that slightly modify the growing cycle to those which are too powerful (such as SO4);

* the replacement in the 1970s of mass selection with cloning—not a particularly successful change; a reversion to the old ways soon intervened;

* the introduction of mechanical harvesting, another rather unconvincing innovation; after trying the machnes, the great vineyards soon reverted to harvesting by hand;

* soil analysis which made it possible to identify and correct any deficiencies;

* extending the practice of sorting the grape harvest immediately, accompanied by a development in the sorting and grading conveyor belt;

* the invention of green harvests;

* the widespread technique of removal of the stalk before the grapes were sent for pressing.

Modern cellar with annular circulation.

* the emergence of what might be termed an ecological reaction, leading to the development of "reasoned cultivation" and "biological cultivation."

The fermentation process

The cellar master and œnologist have both helped to improve the material with which they have to work and have seen a substantial increase in their options, which explains why their importance has increased.

* Trituration of the grape, especially the use of pumps, is no longer necessary.
* Maintenance of the vats has been greatly improved. Tartar and deep-seated bacteria have been eliminated.
* Stainless steel has won the day for storage purposes, although in some cases there has been a return to wooden vats.
* Numerous procedures for regulating temperature have emerged over time.

• Malolactic fermentation, whether encouraged or provoked, has become generalized. The great wines already resorted to it if they required long periods of aging.

• The advent of crioextraction, a controversial practice which is of particular interest to the great sweet white wines.

• The invention of gentle, antioxidant wine-presses that reduce the amount of sediment, is a development from which white wines, in particular, have benefited greatly.

Aging in the Winestore
The importance of new wood is now recognized by everyone—it was always understood by the great wine-makers—as well as the importance of the origin and age of the wood, again something that the great wine-makers were conscious of from the late seventeenth century. The duration of the aging process, another factor in the basic constituents of a fine

Detail
of a vat.

The sap rises,
the vine weeps.
(Burgundy).

wine, remains a question of style, however. The practice of analyzing wines is not an innovation because in the great estates, it has been common practice since the second half of the nineteenth century. Certain new techniques are new and may alter the taste and style of wines, but they are never used to produce great wines. These include carbon-dioxide maceration (used mainly for Beaujolais) and skin contact for white wine grape skins.

Nothing will be said about the various physical or chemical processes whose aim is to cure sick wiles or improve an imperfect balance. Measures include acidification, deacidification, decoloration, and doctoring with tannin. Of course, these evils are totally foreign to the great wines of great vintage years. Nor do great wine-makers have any truck with the new "miracle" yeasts which introduce "foreign flavors" into the wine.

Innovation and progress obviously have organoleptic consequences which clearly make it even harder to produce an objective comparison of wines. More will be said about this later. If they have been introduced it is because they brought a number of advantages with them, but the question could well be put as to who was the real beneficiary. Was it the wine-makers whose work was made easier, more reliable, and more profitable? Or was it the consumers who could "drink better wine for less money"?

No doubt these changes in the culture have enabled wines to be produced to a more consistent standard, giving the grapes better resistance to attacks of mildew and oidium wilt, and thus improving the quality. On one hand, these forms of progress have done little to change the way in which the great wines of the best vintages are created. This is despite the fact that the standardization of the plant material has contributed to the simplifications and uniformity of flavor and odor. On the other hand, the esthetic consequences are immediate in the case of vinification and aging.

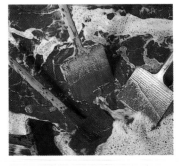

At the turn of the twentieth and beginning of the twenty-first century, the wines being made are far less volatile. They are less sulfurous (especially the sweet white wines), fresher and less dry (in the sense of "ending on a dry note") because the aging process takes much less time (and the old-fashioned methods could also lead to oxidation.)

Thanks to fermentation temperature control, volatile acidity can be avoided as well as aromatic anomalies which could even occur in outstanding years. These are matters that concern us.

All this shows how important it is to bring the consequences of changes in production methods into the equation when comparing vintages produced in a long time ago. Despite the apparent impossibility, such a comparison ought also to take account of the great age of a wine while refusing to make allowances for it. Involving the age of a wine can excuse it for being too young, tolerate it for being too old, and even attempt to imagine or reconstitute the way it was at its apogee. There are so many parameters to be considered… Refusing to be swayed by the age of a wine means judging it as it is today, as it now presents itself and refusing to comment on what it will be or once was. At most, a wine-taster can somehow project himself into the skin and tastebuds of a fellow expert from the period when the wine reached the zenith of perfection. As an example, lovers of early music disagree over whether instruments of the period should be used to play it. In other words, whether or not an attempt should be made to reconstruct the sound as it would have been heard by the contemporaries of the composer.

The experience is possible but valueless. The sounds we hear today blur those which we believe to be "of the period." Our hearing has been distorted, or shaped, as is the palate of the wine-taster, who has never tasted volatile acidity and is unused to oxidation or drying out. A taster who claims to be able to judge a very old wine more or less objectively should consequently imagine it at its apogee and try and reproduce in his mind the taste-sensitivity of the period.

Caution must thus be paramount. Although the greatest wines of the prestigious appellations and the best years are known, this is of little assistance in an attempt to award the title "the best of the best. "There is no one best; there is better. When the top classifications of Premier Cru, Second Cru, and so on, were first introduced for claret in 1855, their creators realized this and specified that there was to be no hierarchy within each class.

Facing page: documents classifying Bordeaux wines, 1855.

Vins blancs classés de la Gironde

Crûs	Communes	Propriétaires

Vins rouges classés du Dépar.t de la Gironde

Crûs	Communes	Propriétaires	(Batrand)

Premiers Crûs

Château Lafite — Pauillac

Bordeaux, le 18 avril 1855

Les Syndic et Adjoints

Des Courtiers de Commerce près la Bourse de Bordeaux.

A Messieurs les Membres de la Chambre

de Commerce de Bordeaux.

Messieurs,

Nous avons eu l'honneur de recevoir votre lettre du 5 de ce mois, par laquelle vous nous demandiez la liste complète des vins rouges classés de la Gironde, ainsi que celle de vos grands vins blancs.

Afin de nous conformer à votre désir, nous nous sommes entourés de tous les renseignements possibles, & nous avons l'honneur de vous faire connaître, par le tableau

Very Great Wines and Archetypal Wines

The Very Great Wines belong to every archetype. How many archetypes are there? How are they created? Why are there some very great wines which do not belong in any of these fixed and recognized categories, or to put it another way, how can a wine be considered great if it is in a category that is not recognized throughout the world?

The Very Great Wines, recognized on an international level, reach this status by means of a mysterious consensus and are universally sought after. This results in their high prices.

Only wines produced in sufficient quantity and belonging to a recognized type, such as Burgundy, Bordeaux, etc., can claim such recognition.

This means that wines that could claim international recognition by virtue of their quality are excluded, since the volume of production is insufficient or they do not belong to an archetype.

It would be ridiculous to believe that the archetypes are fixed and that no new category will ever be created. Yet curiously enough, the so-called "new producers" (countries outside Europe, the case of the United States remaining ambiguous) have never proposed a totally new archetype and are happy to model their products on existing types. These models or archetypes are as follows (the grape varieties are in brackets):

Facing page:
Wine auction at
the Hospices
de Beaune in
Burgundy.

Red wines:

• Bordeaux or similar types,

• Burgundy or similar types,

• Châteauneuf-du-Pape (Grenache).

And to a lesser extent:

• Hermitage (Syrah), Barolo-Barbaresco (Nebbiolo) and Brunello de Montalcino (Sangiovese Grosso) types.

White wines:

• White Burgundy and Chardonnay types,

• Champagne types,

• sweet white wines (all grape varieties).

There remains the case of Sauvignon, a grape variety which is used to make dry and sweet Bordeaux-style wines but which is incapable of being a serious rival to the international Chardonnay archetype.

In the case of dry white wines, the same could be said of Riesling, an equally great variety.

Two grape stocks could contribute the degree of originality that one is entitled to expect from the new producing countries. These are Zinfandel in the United States and Pinotage in South Africa, but neither variety has yet produced wines that can be described as archetypal in the way that the above reds and whites have done.

It is hard to explain why a particular archetype has been adopted on an international level. On the other hand, it is possible to trace the conditions in which they were born. There is no producer without consumers and the natural tendency of all consumers is to diversify production, so as to be able to sell in greater quantity, and produce a better quality, so as to be able to sell the product at a higher price. Expensive wines can only be afforded by wealthy customers, and these are to be found almost exclusively in the big cities of rich, powerful, and organized countries. Throughout history, whenever such conditions have combined, archetypal wines have appeared and have perpetuated their name. Examples of such memorable wines are Mareotic from the days when Cleopatra ruled Egypt, Pramenian or Chio from Ancient Greece, the famous Falernian that Pliny drunk in Rome.

It was not until the Renaissance that new archetypes, such as Tokay in Hungary and Ausbruch in Austria, emerged onto the scene. In the seventeenth century, the great red wines made their appearance. The great categories fixed at that time are those that are still used to this day

Facing page:
Roman fresco from
the Veuve-Clicquot
cellar.

LA VIGNE

(In fact, these wines were much more heavily oxidized and had a volatile acidity which would be rejected nowadays.)

To make a few generalizations, it could be said that the red Burgundies represented the French archetypal red wine (they were drunk by the French king and his court), while the clarets were favored by wealthy Englishmen (and were drunk by the English king and his court). Only the English thought it worth paying the high prices for the wines which today we call Premiers Crus.

It is a strange phenomenon that the archetypes have hardly changed at all in four centuries, while the food which accompanies the wine has changed so radically.

As always, in art as in wine, the canon law of esthetics was determined by the dominant power or powers. Yet we continue to classify wines along the old lines despite the fact that the United States is now the dominant world power. It can be imagined that in the twenty-first century the emerging countries of southeast Asia will become the arbiters of fashion, in wine as in everything else.

So what will become of our traditional models?

Œnophiles are already speaking of "American taste," which can be summarized briefly as wines that are more woody and powerful, sometimes at the expense of finesse.

Facing page: wine and high society.
Dining-room of the *Ritz Hotel,* Paris.

Traditional Wine-producing Countries

France

Despite some assertions, it is unlike that the Celts who occupied France ever made wine. On the other hand, it is admitted that the Greeks and Romans introduced viticulture into all the countries with which they had a relationship, whether through trading or occupation.

Vineyards spread through the Midi and the Rhone Valley of France even before the Christian era.

By the thirteenth century, vines could be found throughout France, but it took six centuries for the right grape varieties to be planted in the right locations, the last one being Merlot, introduced into Medoc, in the mid-nineteenth century.

The archetypes referred to here were born during this long period. Some are very ancient. The current Côtes Rotie/Hermitage may well be very similar to the *vinum picantum* which the Romans imported from Vienne (twenty centuries ago), but the Burgundy type is "only" six centuries old, Bordeaux as we know it today is 150 years old and brut Champagne has been around for barely a century

The first half of the century witnessed the birth of the *Appellations d'Origine Contrôlée* and the second half saw the emergence of a profession "invented" in the last nineteenth century, but which is now vital to the trade. The twentieth century can be divided into two very distinct periods, the first from 1900 through 1965 when the vineyard "survived," and the second, from 1965 to the end of the century, which flourishes like the golden age of the nineteenth century (1850-1880).

Facing page:
Winestore master,
Château d'Yquem,
1921.

Bordeaux, clarets

Bordeaux has the largest growing area in the world for fine wines (110,000 hectares), and remains a model for France and the rest of the world. From the mid-seventeenth century, Bordeaux invented "the great wine" which the British hastened to adopt. Bordeaux-type wines are imitated in the French Midi, in Italy, Spain, the United States and the new wine-producing countries. In the category of great vintages, which is what we are concerned with here, 1961 for example, Bordeaux remains unequaled. Apart from these exceptional vintages, numerous blind tasting have revealed that there are plenty of "imitators" which are at least the equal of the original.

Burgundy reds

The Bordeaux grape varieties possess great plasticity, unlike Pinot Noir, which is choosy, fastidious, and difficult to please. So far, the Burgundy-type wines produced outside the Côte-d'Or of Burgundy are the equal to the local premiers crus but the very great grands crus (Romanée-Conti, Richebourg, Chambertin from the best growers, for instance) remain unrivaled. That may be because for the past eight centuries, Burgundy has made a virtue of isolating very small parcels of land of a particularly high quality which has never been equaled.

Burgundy whites

The plasticity of Chardonnay is only equaled by that of Cabernet Sauvignon, as long as temperatures remain moderate. It has been said and written that the great white Burgundies were unsurpassed. This fact is confirmed less and less, however, by blind tastings.

Châteauneuf-du-Pape

This wine has an international reputation which is even higher than its reputation in France. The grape variety from which it is made is mainly Grenache, and it is true to say that the wine has neither imitators nor competitors.

Preceding pages:
The Gironde river
from the
Château Latour
estate.

Syrah wines

Tasters differ in their opinions. In this sector, however, new producers such as Australia, are beginning to produce wines of a quality comparable with those of the French models.

Champagne

France was the inventor of sparkling wines. Despite the fact that it is inimitable, champagne is copied everywhere, even in France, in regions which boast of having produced fizzy wine even before Champagne itself (Limoux, Die, and others). Champagne owes its quality and specificity to the land and the northern aspect of the 30,000 ha vineyard from which it comes, as well as to the fact that the varieties of grape used to make it are restricted to Chardonnay, Pinot Noir (for the very great wines) and Pinot Meunier. The best Champagnes are of an incomparable finesse. Paradoxically, the production of genuine Champagne is small (about 300 million bottles) compared to worldwide production of the other sparkling wines, and even the production of the two Spanish giants, Freixenet and Cordoniu.

France	
Area of Vineyard:	825,000 ha
Production :	51 million hl
Main grape varieties:	
Reds	• Cabernet Sauvignon
	• Merlot
	• Pinot Noir
	• Syrah
	• Grenache
	• Carignan
Whites	• Chardonnay
	• Chenin
	• Sauvignon Blanc
Export:	
	• United States
	• United Kingdom
	• Benelux countries
	• Switzerland
	• Japan

Germany

Germany is a country with a very ancient wine-making tradition. It remains to be discovered whether Mosel wine was first made eighteen centuries ago or only fourteen.

One thing it certain, namely that it was not the Romans who introduced the grape varieties that are able to cope with the colder climate, because they were only familiar with "southern" stocks. It is likely that a native wild grape was tamed and selected. There is every reason to believe that the vine in question was a Riesling, although this variety is not mentioned until the fifteenth century. The fixing of German-type wines therefore dates from ancient times. The sweet type appeared in the seventeenth century. In 1775, Johann Engert, steward of the Schloss Johannisberg, wrote to the Abbot-Prince Fulda, owner of the estate, describing the 1775 vintage as being extraordinary.

History (or perhaps legend, since the same story is told about Yquem) relates that Engert harvested grapes that had rotted on the vine that year because permission to pick them had arrived too late.

The syrupy, sweet white wines which were the result were all the rage in the nineteenth century. They then fell out of favor, and it was not until 1921 (still known as the "year of the century") that a magnificent Trockenbeerenauslese was vinified.

After World War II, these sweet white wines rotted by the botrytis fungus became greatly sought after by œnophiles and became the most expensive wines in the world.

The regulations governing German wines, which fortunately were simplified in 1971 are among the very few which are not based on the French system. Although, like the French system, it defines wine-growing districts, but otherwise it regulates the sugar content of the must.

Preceding pages: vines in the snow in the Épernay district.
Facing page: many historic vineyards are of Roman origin.
Here, a Roman ship is transporting wine.

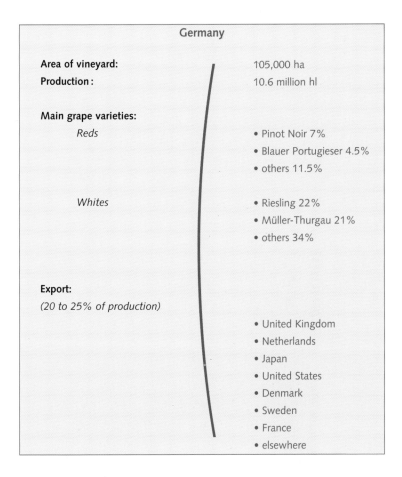

Germany

Area of vineyard: 105,000 ha
Production: 10.6 million hl

Main grape varieties:
    Reds
                                       • Pinot Noir 7%
                                       • Blauer Portugieser 4.5%
                                     • others 11.5%

    Whites
                                       • Riesling 22%
                                     • Müller-Thurgau 21%
                                     • others 34%

Export:
(20 to 25% of production)
                                     • United Kingdom
                                     • Netherlands
                                     • Japan
                                     • United States
                                     • Denmark
                                     • Sweden
                                     • France
                                     • elsewhere

Austria

Vines have been grown in Austria since Roman times. Austrian reds have character and are produced from local varieties of grape (Saint-Laurent, Lemberg), but few are exported. As a result of scandals involving noxious chemical additives, Austria has produced very strict legislation governing wines. Sweet white wines have achieved international renown, which ought not to surprise the connoisseurs who have long placed them in the first rank of the wines made from grapes subject to "noble rot" or botrytis.

Hungary

The historic Hungarian vineyard is also of Roman origin and reached the

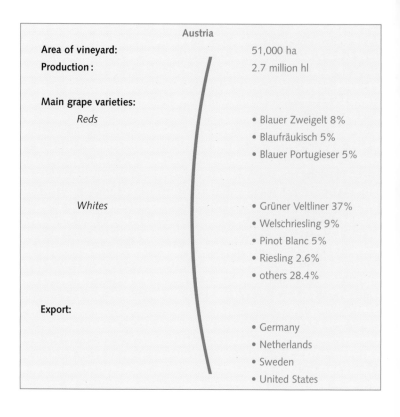

Austria

Area of vineyard:	51,000 ha
Production:	2.7 million hl

Main grape varieties:

Reds
- Blauer Zweigelt 8%
- Blaufräukisch 5%
- Blauer Portugieser 5%

Whites
- Grüner Veltliner 37%
- Welschriesling 9%
- Pinot Blanc 5%
- Riesling 2.6%
- others 28.4%

Export:
- Germany
- Netherlands
- Sweden
- United States

height of its glory when grapes were harvested late and began to suffer from the "noble rot". Within a matter of a few years, Tokay became the wine drunk at court. The Hapsburgs even produced their own Tokay in their own vineyard. In Russia, the Tsar himself went wild over it. Rákóczi, the count, prince and great landowner (who also had a vineyard in Tokay) enabled Louis XIV to discover it in the early eighteenth century. In 1816, Julien classified it as being among the two or three best wines in the world. In the twentieth century, this wine of kings virtually disappeared in the long night of Communism—like civilizations wines are mortal. In South Africa, political and administrative incompetence had already killed off Constancia, Tokay's great rival in the nineteenth century and the favorite wine of Napoleon and Louis-Philippe. It was at an opportune moment that the Communist economy foundered and the system of state farms ended, since it had proved incapable of vinifying a fine wine. Today, Tokay is an archetypal sweet white wine.

Preceding pages:
vineyard in the fall in the Rust region of Austria.

Facing page:
Eszencia, the rare and precious wine produced in the Tokay region of Hungary.

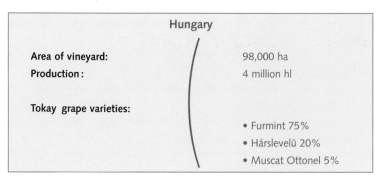

Hungary

Area of vineyard: 98,000 ha
Production :   4 million hl

Tokay grape varieties:

• Furmint 75%
• Hárslevelü 20%
• Muscat Ottonel 5%

Italy

The collapse of the Roman Empire brought about the disappearance of the great Roman wines.

For many centuries, the Italians concentrated on producing cheap wines for local consumption. It was not until the late nineteenth century that Italy once again found its place among the countries producing great vintages of exceptional quality.

The very great diversity of Italian wines made the task of the legislator more complex, but regulations inspired by the French system were introduced (AOC = DOCG). The first version of the legislation was heavily amended in 1992. No doubt further amendments or adaptations will be made.

Although the return to the production of quality wines began more than a hundred years ago, it was not until the 1970s that this rebirth of the Italian vineyard began to bear fruit, to such an extent that from a historical point of view, Italy could well be classified among the new wine-producing countries.

Portugal

This is another vineyard that owes its origin to the Romans but the Portuguese did not discover the true worth of their grapes until the eighteenth century, when port was invented, almost by chance.

In order to better preserve red wines which were exported, spirits were added to them. It was soon discovered that red wine treated in this way was much more than mere red wine *plus* spirits. That is how port wine was born.

Italy

Area of vineyard:	830,000 ha
Production:	55 million hl

Main grape varieties:
(great diversity – 400 varieties)

Reds
- Sangiovese
- Nebbiolo
- Cabernet Sauvignon
- Merlot

Whites
- Trebbiano
- Vernacchia

Export:
(34% of production)

- United States
- United Kingdom
- Benelux countries
- Germany

Facing:
the village
of Montalcino,
in Tuscany, whose
vines produce
Brunello wine.

Portugal

Area of vineyard: 260,000 ha
                                                        (*less than 20% in use*)

Production :   125 million bottles

Main grape varieties:
    Reds   • Touriga Nacional
                                                        • Touriga Francesa
                                                        • Tinta Roriz
                                                        • Tinta Barreca
                                                        • Tinto Cao

    Whites   • Gouveio (Gouvelo)
                                                        • Malvasia Fino

Export:
(*about 80 % of production*)
Regular port wines:
                                                        • France 34%
                                                        • Netherlands 17%
                                                        • Benelux countries 14%
                                                        • others 35%
Finest port wines:
                                                        • United Kingdom 35.2%
                                                        • United States 15.2%
                                                        • France 10.7%
                                                        • others 38.9%

Preceding pages: old vintage bottles of Brunello di Montalcino,
preserved in La Tenuta Greppo.
Facing page: cellar containing vintage port, Portugal.

New Producers

The United States

To include the United States, or even the American continent, among the ranks of new producers is historically questionable because the conquistadors and Spanish missionaries introduced European grape varieties into Mexico in the sixteenth century, and these later spread northward and southward.

Grapevines and wine have had a certain amount of bad luck in the United States. Thomas Jefferson imported great vine stocks from Burgundy and Bordeaux in the early nineteenth century, which he had taken from vineyards that he knew well (he had bought wine from such prestigious estates as Yquem, Latour, Lafite, and Montrachet), and this should have been the birth of American viticulture. But that was without taking account of phylloxera, the plant-lice whose existence had been unknown hitherto, and which attacked the roots of the European grapes (*vitis vinifera*), doing little damage to the native American vines (*vitis lambrusca*) which had built up some immunity to them.

In the late nineteenth century, the Americans were producing quality wines. They proved to be more than a match for European wines at the Paris exhibitions and won medals. At the time, there were more than eight hundred growers in California.

Then came Prohibition (1919-1933), followed by the economic crisis and World War II. This explains why it was not until the late 1960s that œnophiles began to take an interest in American wines.

Since then, American production has won its letters of nobility, and is popular locally as well as internationally. Blind taste tests of American wines produced from Chardonnay or Cabernet-Merlot grapes are the equal of the best European wines.

United States

Area of vineyard: 135,000 ha
Production: 2.5 million tons of grapes

Main grape varieties:

Reds
- Zinfandel 13%
- Cabernet Sauvignon 13%
- Merlot 4.5%
- Grenache 4.5%

Whites
- Chardonnay 23.5%
- Colombard 20.5%
- Chenin Blanc 11%
- Sauvignon Blanc 4.5%
- Muscat 4%
- Riesling 1.5%

Exportation:
(90% of production exported is from California)

- United Kingdom 23.5%
- Japan 19%
- Canada 17%
- Netherlands 7.5%
- Switzerland 4.5%
- France 2%
- others 26.5%

Spain

Spain is not a new producer of wines but it is a new producer of top quality wines.

The history of Spanish viticulture is not dissimilar to the Italian experience. Once again, it was the Romans who introduced the art of wine into the Iberian peninsula. Eight centuries of Islamic rule, however, did not encourage the production of wine, nor did the feudal system of land management which persisted long after the Middle Ages.

However, in the mid-nineteenth century, a few growers revived viticulture in the Rioja region by introducing methods as well as grape varieties from the Bordeaux district. They grew mainly Grenache as well as a local variety, the Tempranillo. It was a wine made from the latter variety that won the Marquess of Riscal first prize at the great wine competition organized in 1865 in Bordeaux. The diseases of the vine from which France was suffering at the time contributed to orienting viticulture in Rioja toward basic wines of good average quality. It was not until after World War II that modern, rational œnology opened the gates of international markets. Curiously, it is not in Rioja but further to the southwest, on the banks of the Duero, that is the birthplace of the great post-war Spanish wines which have taken their place among the ranks of the world's outstanding vintages.

Of course, Spanish production was already world-famous in the nineteenth century for its fortified wines, Malaga and Sherry.

Preceding pages: vineyard in the Napa Valley, California.
Facing page: the Vega Sicilia bodega, Valbuena de Duero, Spain.

Spain

Area of vineyard:	1.328 million ha of which 650,000 are in a DO (*Denominación d'Origen*)
Production:	29.7 million hl of which 9.6 are from the DOs
Main grape varieties:	
Reds	• Grenache Noir • Bobal • Tempranillo
Whites	• Airén • Pedro Ximenes
Export:	• Germany • United Kingdom • France • United States • Netherlands

Left and right:
Vega Sicilia
vineyard, Valbuena
de Duero.

Australia

This country is a special case. Vines were not introduced until the nineteenth century and no local variety has been developed.

A long wine-making tradition has often been an obstacle to innovation. In Australia, there is no such obstacle, so wine-making has always incorporated the latest growing methods and production techniques, to such a point that Australian œnologists were the first to become professional international consultants.

These *flying winemakers* even vinified in France. It should be stated, however, that French œnologists have since caught up with them and are dispensing their advice in the four corners of the earth! Australia is now one of the countries which is producing wine of the finest quality. This is due to the wide range of climate types, a variety of soils and aspects, enormous opportunities for expansion, and complete mastery of the vinification techniques. Large financial resources are there to back up the wine trade enabling Australia to produce the finest vintages. Australia may be inspired by the achievements of New Zealand, which has already produced a wine with an international reputation, Cloudy Bay, made from Sauvignon Blanc grapes.

Australia	
Area of vineyard:	88,000 ha
Production:	3 million hl
Main grape varieties:	
Reds	• Cabernet Sauvignon
	• Merlot
	• Pinot Noir
Whites	• Chardonnay
	• Riesling
Export:	
(25% of production)	
	• United States 34%
	• United Kingdom 32%
	• Denmark 37%

Facing and subsequent pages: vineyards of the Barossa Valley, Australia.

Producers of Tomorrow

Chile

The late Professor Enjalbert, a geographer from the Bordeaux region who specialized in identifying the best wine-growing environments, always maintained that Chile had the greatest possible wine-growing potential. Although Professor Enjalbert has been dead for some years, the great Chilean wine, of a stature capable of rivaling Lafite and Latour has yet to make its appearance.

Chile produces excellent wines but none has hitherto been able to compete with the greatest in the world. This is hard to figure out, when you take account of the fact that the local climate is perfect, tempered by the Pacific Ocean and cooled by the cold night air from the Andes while benefiting from plenty of sunshine. As far as the geology is concerned, the siliceous or clay-and-limestone soils are very well drained. Furthermore, the plethora of valleys at right angles to the coast create microclimates and aspects that are very favorable to grape-growing. If Chile has not yet produced great wines, this may be due to a superabundance of favorable conditions which have resulted in a huge harvest, encouraging the production of wines that are easy to sell. What Chile lacks is the small, enthusiastic grower who is passionate about wine, has plenty of funds at his disposal, and is determined to produce a masterpiece. One will emerge sooner or later.

The country has never experienced the phylloxera plague but most of the grapes grown are of an old, local variety, the País, plus a few of the great European grapes.

Chile

Area of vineyard:	63,500 ha
Production:	4.5 million hl

Main grape varieties:

Reds	• Cabernet Sauvignon 24%
	• Merlot 8%
	• Pinot Noir 5%
Whites	• Chardonnay 8%
	• Sauvignon Blanc 10%
	• Riesling 4%
	• Chenin 1%
	• Sémillion 1%
Local varieties:	• País
	• Others
Export:	
	• United States
	• United Kingdom
	• Japan
	• Canada
	• Denmark

Facing: Errazuriz, a Chilean cellar.

Following pages: Vina Undurraga, a Chilean wine.

South Africa

The first wine produced in South Africa was drunk in February, 1659, when Louis XIV had been king of France for about twenty years. Since then, South African wine has been through some chaotic times. The creation of a national cooperative (KWV) in 1918 did not bring about the hoped-for innovations and improvements, with the exception of the invention, in 1926, of the Pinotage variety, the result of crossing a Pinot Noir and a Cinsault. In 1973, a system similar to the French AOC system, called *Wine of Origin* (WO), was created.

Apartheid took a heavy toll on exports and isolated South African viticulture but it is now emerging from that situation and is starting over in the production of great wines.

South Africa

Area of vineyard: 101,000 ha
Production: 55 million hl

Main grape varieties:

Reds
- Cabernet Sauvignon 13%
- Merlot 5.6%
- Pinotage 5.4%
- others 11%

Whites
- Chenin Blanc 23%
- Sauvignon Blanc 15%
- Chardonnay 10%
- Cape Riesling (Crouchen Blanc) 7%
- others 10%

Export:
(22% of production)
- United Kingdom 40%
- Netherlands 13%
- Germany 8.5%
- Scandinavia 7%
- France 2.5%
- others 29%

Facing page: winestore of the Plaisir-de-Merle estate at Franschoek, South Africa.

Following pages: vineyard of the Thelema estate at Stellenbosch, South Africa.

New Zealand

Grapevines were introduced into New Zealand in 1819, by the Reverend Samuel Marsden, a missionary who brought a few plants from Australia. Phylloxera first made an appearance in 1895, no doubt for the same reason as it did in Europe, namely the importation of American vines. For many years, New Zealand produced poor-quality wines from hybrid varieties, then white wines from German varieties and finally, excellent white wines made from Sauvignon and Chardonnay grapes.

This talent for producing good white wines is due to the coolness of the climate. The delay in producing quality wines was due largely to the prohibitionists, whose activity reached a peak in the 1930s. They managed to achieve a ban on the sale of wine in most public places, including restaurants! Wine could not be sold in supermarkets until as recently as 1989. However, all that is in the past and future now belongs to New Zealand viticulture.

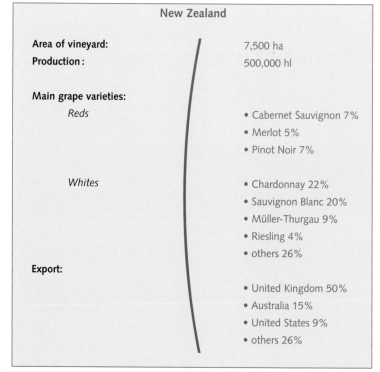

New Zealand

Area of vineyard: 7,500 ha
Production: 500,000 hl

Main grape varieties:
Reds
- Cabernet Sauvignon 7%
- Merlot 5%
- Pinot Noir 7%

Whites
- Chardonnay 22%
- Sauvignon Blanc 20%
- Müller-Thurgau 9%
- Riesling 4%
- others 26%

Export:
- United Kingdom 50%
- Australia 15%
- United States 9%
- others 26%

Facing page: vineyard on the Omaka Springs property, Marlborough, New Zealand.

Following pages: Pinot Noir grapes before sorting for pressing, Montana property, New Zealand.

Second Part
Vintages of the Century

1900

Naturally, the advent of the twentieth century was celebrated in style. A few party-poopers who insisted that the nineteenth century actually lasted until December 31, 1900 because the first year of the century had ended on December 31, 1800, few people took any notice of them. The year 1900 was an eventful one for France. It was the year when the first Metro (subway) line was opened, between the Porte Maillot and the Porte de Vincennes. The entrances, designed by Hector Guimard, have become classic examples of the Art Nouveau style.

The Paris Universal Exposition offered a glimpse of the future. There was brilliant electric lighting, cinematography in every shape and form including a movie theater called the Cinéorama with a completely circular screen, Louis Lumière's giant screen and the Phonorama, an early forerunner of the talkies.

Many of the exhibition buildings at the lower end of the Champs-Élysées have lasted the whole century. They include the Petit-Palais and Grand-Palais, as well as the Alexander III Bridge over the Seine.

Nietzsche died while, in Vienna, a certain Dr. Freud discreetly published a book on the subject of the interpretation of dreams. Max Planck, in Germany, disputed the theory of energy waves proving that energy is distributed discontinuously in the form of "grains" which he called "quanta." The painter Claude Monet exhibited his series of ten Impressionist paintings called The Waterlillies.

Facing page:
18th century map
of Margaux.

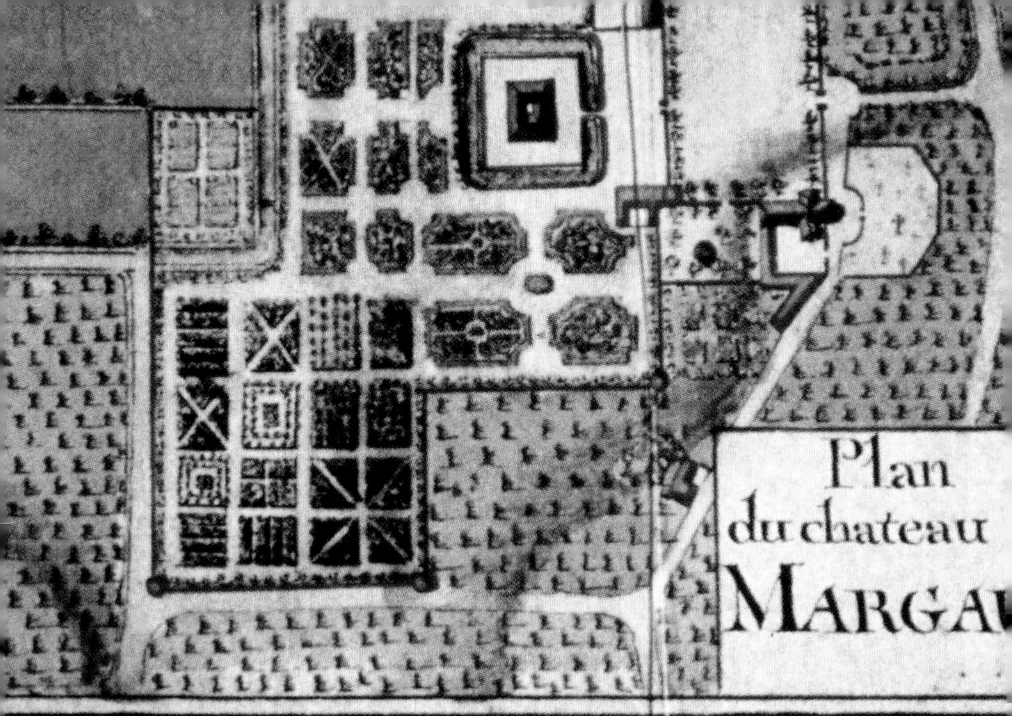

Plan
du chateau
MARGA

Margaud est une tresbelle maison q
De Beaux jardins Son Seigneur a ma
quantité de vins et L'on tient quil e
fait quelque fois pour plus de cinquan
mille livres par an.

Les Vignes de ceo quartiers sont echala
avec des Echalats comme au Avrus de
paris, et non celles de Saintonge q

Château Margaux 1900 Bordeaux

Château Margaux was very quick to learn from Haut-Brion and was sold on the British market, under its own name, from the early eighteenth century. This was especially easy to achieve since these two pioneering estates were linked by ties of marriage. Jean-Denis d'Aulède, owner of the Château Margaux, had married Thérèse de Pontac, whose father was the owner of Haut-Brion.

In the seventeenth century, Château Margaux added a building block to the historic creation of a "great wine" in the Bordeaux sense of the term, when the manager of the estate, Berlon, recommended separating white grapevines from red and produced red wines solely from red grapes and white wines solely from white grapes.

Opposite: old vintages in storage at the Château Margaux.

The estate changed hands several times. Certain owners were rather eccentric (and wealthy) such as the one who built the château (1810), no doubt to confirm his being ennobled with the title of marquess. Later, the estate came into the ownership of the bankers Aguado (1836) and Pillet-Will (1879). The latter undertook the replanting of the estate after the devastation caused by philloxera. Under his aegis, the memorable vintages of 1899 and 1900 were vinified.

Pillet-Will's son-in-law was one of the most eccentric owners of the property. There was no question of his noble lineage, his blood was of the bluest; he was a Tremoille, and a duke to boot.

But his politics were—of the Left and he was known as the Red Duke! This was not a good time for the property, however, and the duke was forced to hand it over Château Margaux to agents, who badly

mishandled its affairs. When the Ginestet family bought the estate, they nurtured a proposal, one that was wise but heartily condemned by wine buffs, to sell non-vintage Château Margaux wines. The project was abandoned, however.

In 1970, the American firm of National Distillers made a bid for Château Margaux. Bordeaux wines were experiencing a crisis, but a Premier Cru had to remain French and the government decided to oppose the sale. It was the owner of the Félix Potin grocery store chain, André Mentzelopoulos, who finally bought the estate.

He invested large sums of money but his shrewdest move was to hire Émile Peynaud, who became the most famous œnologist of the Château. His first vintage (1978) was a triumph. Since then, Château Margaux has maintained its high level, although it is no longer a piece of French heritage, since the Italian Agnelli family control the company.

Château Margaux 1900 is, without a doubt, the finest vintage of the estate. It is also the most highly esteemed by those who know it well, such as Bernard Ginestet and Paul Pontallier, the current house œnologist of Château Margaux.

Perhaps it was in honor of this vintage that Ernest Hemmingway insisted that his granddaughter be named for the prestigious wine of the Margaux estate.

The grape harvest
at Château
Margaux.

Organoleptic Description

The robe has developed. It remains fine, though brownish when seen in the mass. The delicate aromas of burnt toast are evidence of the perfect ripening of the grape. It has a smooth harmony in the mouth, melting though now a little old-fashioned (the tannins are on the verge of separating out). In the 1970s, this wine of infinite grace was a symbol of the flower of civilization, the crowning glory of Margaux.

Secrets of quality

Balance and successful vinification.

Apogee
1920.

Availability

Very rare.

Comparable, or almost comparable, vintages: 1947, 1953, 1961.

Current price

FF 10,000 (1,525 euros) –a bottle fetched FF 50,000 at an auction in 1999.

Development: beginning to decline.

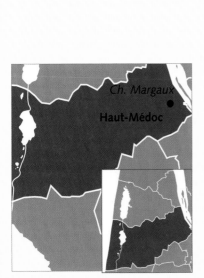

Ch. Margaux
Haut-Médoc

Weather Conditions

In 1900, spring and summer were ideal for grape-growing. There were no problems with flowering, so the harvest was abundant. In this respect, 1900 is closer to 1982 than it is to 1921 or 1961. Everything went well, just as it had the previous year. The wines were excellent, balanced but not of consistent quality. At the time, some of the brokers discovered that a few of them had been diluted.

1

2

1. *Waterlillies*
Claude Monet exhibits a series of ten canvases in Paris.

2.**The Alexander III Bridge**
Its construction was completed for the opening of the Universal Exposition in Paris.

3. *The Interpretation of Dreams*
Publication of Sigmund Freud's seminal work in Austria.

4. **1900 style**
One of the many entrances designed in by Hector Guimard to the Métropolitain, the first subway line in Paris.

5. **Friedrich Nietzsche**
Death of the German philosopher.

1911

Another Franco-German war was narrowly avoided. All this in the name of colonial balance. The crisis point came when the German battleship *Panther* anchored in the port of Agadir, Morocco. Although the 1906 agreement was supposed to guarantee Moroccan independence, it was only partially complied with because in May, French troops restored order in Fez. It was claimed in Paris that this was at the request of the Sultan. Negotiations between Germany and France ended in November with an accord that recognized Morocco as having the status of a French protectorate. In exchange, France ceded to Germany nearly 300,000 sq. km. of the French Congo, which were incorporated into the German colony of Cameroon. Simultaneously, at the opposite ends of the earth, the Manchurian dynasty lost control of most of China.

The Chinese Republic, which became a dictatorship, was officially proclaimed in 1912.

In Great Britain, George V was crowned king.

In the arts, 1911 saw the foundation of the famous French publisher, Gallimard, and the creation of the ballet *Petrushka,* with music by Stravinsky, by Diaghilev's Ballets Russes. Ernest Rutherford published his theory that the atom was not a homogenous particle but consisted of a nucleus, surrounded by electrons. Marie Curie won her second Nobel Prize, this time for chemistry, and the discovery of radium and polonium. She had won the Nobel Prize for Physics in 1903.

Facing page:
ancient bottles
of Bollinger
champagne with
stapled corks.

1911

Bollinger 1911 Champagne

The author asks the reader's indulgence for introducing a personal reminiscence. A few years ago, at the end of a meal at the Bollinger establishment in Ay, we were supposed to be treated to a Bollinger 1914. Probably the cellar that contained the ancient bottles had muted lighting, because in fact the bottle that was opened was a 1911. I was delighted, almost moved.

Delighted, because the 1911 is far superior to the 1914 and it is well-known that no champagne has attained this level of quality since 1874, when the yield per hectare was very low because a frost had descended

Facing page: souvenirs from the house of Bollinger.

on the vineyard and lasted uninterruptedly from May 1 through 22, severely damaging the flowering; the subsequent summer was perfect. Moved, because 1911 was the year of the Champagne riots. At Ay, on 22 April, 1911, six thousand vine-growers faced up to four squadrons of six hundred horsemen, who were brandishing sabers because they had been given an order not to fire. Nothing could stop the rioters. They pillaged and burned everything that stood in their path, setting fire to homes and warehouses, then took the road that led to the Bollinger estate. It is said that the rioters were overcome with respect for the venerable establishment, and turned back. More likely is the theory that it was late in the day and the most turbulent of the rioters were overcome with fatigue.

The reason for these disturbances was the cumulative effect of two phenomena which rendered the situation of the local wine-makers unbearable. The first, known as "the fraud," was the making of

POSTES

RÉPUBLIQUE FRANÇAISE

5c

RÉVOLUTION EN

AY

Hautvillers 2t f...
Hélè...

MPAGNE - AVRIL 1911

estants et Dragons

"champagne" from grapes grown outside the region, enraging the local growers (although there was no AOC for champagne at the time). The second was the clumsiness of French politicians. Although they had introduced a law on February 10, 1911 that specified that only grapes from the area beside the River Marne and known as "Marne" had the right to use the magic name of champagne, they were considering revoking the decision (proceedings of the Senate, April 11, 1911). This is all that was needed to ignite the powder-keg. Shortly thereafter, the politicians committed a further gaffe by placing the Aube district outside the "Champagne" area. The growers stopped paying taxes and more than six thousand of them demonstrated in Troyes. Paris took fright: a commission recommended incorporating Aube into the Champagne district. Continuing to act with crassness, the legislators invented a new appellation: "champagne de seconde zone" (Decree of June 7, 1911). It was not until the end of World War I that good sense prevailed. The tension was so great that from spring through fall, 1911, 40,000 men under the command of seven colonels occupied the vineyards. The army did not leave until after the harvest, spending a most uncomfortable summer in the searing heat. In July, all-time records were broken.

The house of Bollinger was founded in 1829 and remains family-owned and independent. Today, the vineyard covers more than 120 hectares. In 1911, the planted area, which has since been greatly extended, embraced the communes of Cuis, Ay, Verzenay, Louvois, Tauxières and Bouzy. In 1955,

Above:
Jacques Bollinger
(1838), founder
of the firm of
Bollinger.

Preceding pages:
rioting in
Champagne, 1911.

Bollinger launched the "RD" ("récemment dégorgés") series, with the date of the removal of sediment indicated on a special label on the opposite side of the bottle. In 1969, the very rare "Bollinger vieilles vignes françaises", a *blanc de noir* produced from two (and recently three) small plots of ungrafted vines. There are 30,000 plants to the hectare, the harvest is trodden underfoot as in the eighteenth century. Careful vinification, fermentation in the bottle, *tirage* on the cork, and a long time on the lees.

Organoleptic Description

Once the wire had been removed, the cork did not resist being pulled. It was stapled in place, the wine having popped it many years previous. Yet contrary to all expectations, the wine still contained gas. It was not "bubbling," but full of tiny bubbles which rose constantly to the surface. They streaked a uniform yellow robe which contained no shadows or browning. The wine was ripe without being old, the balance was perfect because there was still a measure of acidity but oxidation. The aromas which emerged were lemony and slightly candied with a hint of hazelnut, long, subtle symphony. It all goes to disprove what one often hears said: "Champagne is not a wine."

Secrets of quality

Exceptionally hot weather, grapes ripening with acidity.

Availability

None.

Current price

Not on the market.

Apogee probably around **1925-1930.**

Comparable, or almost comparable, vintages: 1921, 1928, 1937, 1947, 1953, 1961.

Development: when the cork can no longer retain the gas, it will not be champagne.

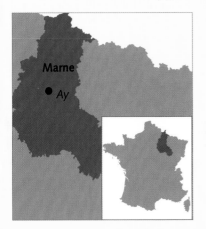

Weather Conditions

Early harvesting, around September 10, in magnificent weather, sent the soldiers back to barracks. The harvest did not last long because there were so few grapes, only 1,600 kilograms per hectare (as against an average harvest of 12,000 today!). Even for the period this was a poor yield, there was no need to pick over the grapes which were in perfect condition.

4

5

1. The British Royal Family
King George V, shown here soon after his coronation on a trip to India.

2. Fall of Manchurian Dynasty in China
This was the beginning of the Republic of China which was proclaimed in 1912 and soon became a dictatorship.

3. The Ballets Russes
Illustration from the first decade of the century, the fabulous era which saw the triumph of Igor Stravinsky, Serge Diaghilev, Vaslav Nijinsky and Leon Bakst.

4. Moroccan Independence
Occupation of Fez by French troops during the fight with the Germans.

5. Rioting in Champagne
On April 22, six thousand wine-makers demonstrated in Ay to protest against "fraud," the use of grapes from outside the region to make Champagne.

1921

Hitler proclaims himself president of the NSDAP (National Socialist German Workers Party—the Nazis) on July 29, 1921; Mussolini makes the Fascist Party the official party of government, taking the title of *Duce* ("leader"); Hirohito, son of the Emperor of Japan, rules as regent from 1921 through 1926, acceding to the imperial throne on his father's death. In China, Mao Zedong helps to form the Chinese Communist Party.

In the aftermath of World War I, there are endless negotiations over the reparations owed by Germany to France. The German economy is in crisis, the German mark is massively devalued.

Spanish Morocco rebels against Spain, under the leadership of Abd el-Krim. The British attempt to establish a protectorate in Persia, where oil production is on the increase, through General Riza Khan. In the same year, southern Ireland is granted home rule and Great Britain recognizes the Irish Free State. Northern Ireland obtains the status of a dominion.

There are great advances in medicine with the discovery of insulin and introduction of the BCG vaccination. It is the year of the first helicopter flight, the first aerial photograph of Paris, the first freeway (in Berlin) and the invention of wireless telegraphy. A certain Walt Disney produces his first cartoon film. Georges Feydeau and the composer Saint-Saëns die in Paris, Caruso in Naples. Anatole France wins the Nobel Prize for Literature. Henri Landru, "the French Bluebeard," is tried for murdering his wives.

Facing page: bottle of Romanée-Conti.

1921

Romanée-Conti 1921 Burgundy

The Pinot Noir grapes from which this wine is made were planted by
Claude Cousin in 1584, that is 337 years before the harvest of 1921.
This is a unique case, because all the rest of the French vines were
replanted after the philloxera epidemic, between 1880 and 1910.
Romanée-Conti, which had been regularly treated with sulfur carbonate
to protect it from the attacks of the dreaded plant-lice. (This practice
continued until 1945, when the vines were uprooted, which is why
there is no Romanée-Conti wine between 1946 and 1951.)

The Pinot vines were pure French stock and were not grafted but were

Opposite: ancient
vintage bottles of
Romanée-Conti.

propagated by layering. A branch was buried in the earth to enable it to
take root. It is thus indisputable that the Pinot planted in 1584 is
actually and genetically the same one that fruited in 1921.
When Claude Cousin bought the vineyard from the Benedictine
Monastery of Saint-Vivant de Vergy in the Hautes-Côtes district of
Burgundy it covered an area of five journals. The plot was sometimes
referred to as "Cloux des cinq journaux" ("cloux" means "enclosure"
and a journal was a measurement roughly equivalent to 857 acres).
It was later called "Cros des Cloux," meaning "Hollow of the
Enclosures," a hollow indicating a slight dip in the slope at the bottom
of the vineyard.
The famous vineyard passed in succession to the Croonembourg family
and mysteriously acquired the name of Romanée, used for several
vineyards in the area. It is not known if this is a late allusion to Roman
presence in the area or a distortion of the old word "romenie," which is

a reference to a wine which was of legendary quality, produced in the Isles of Greece.

In 1760, Louis-François de Bourbon, Prince de Conti, acquired the Romanée for 92,400 sovereigns, a handsome sum, about ten times the price achieved by neighboring vineyards!

Until the French Revolution, Romanée was never sold but was reserved for the Prince's table. When national treasures were sold off, the prince's name was tuck on the end of Romanée. The revolutionaries must have considered that the aristocratic provenance of the estate was a powerful sales pitch in itself, despite their egalitarian views.

Romanée-Conti fell into the hands of speculators for a time, but this ended when Ouvrard acquired the Romanée-Conti estate and the neighboring Clos de Vougeot, in 1818. He kept the vineyards for 43 years, until his death. His children did not follow his example: Romanée-Conti was sold in 1868, then again in 1869 this time to a Mr Duvault-

Edmond Gaudin, estate manager from the second decade of the century until 1942.

Blochet, a wine merchant from Santenay. Since then, half the estate has belonged to his descendants, the other half having been sold in 1942 to Henri Leroy, a wine merchant. The two families run Romanée-Conti jointly through a company that also manages other grands crus, Such as La Tâche (Monopole), Grands Échezeaux, Richebourg and some of the Montrachets.

Until 1989, the grapes harvested were trodden underfoot in the time-honored way. The stalks are not discarded which generally increases the potential for aging in the wine. The wine is fermented in open vats (with added yeast) and then aged in new bottles. It is only drawn off once (so left on the lees for a long time) and clarified with egg white. When tasted a few years ago, it showed no sign of weakness.

Organoleptic Description

The robe is opaque, brightly colored, and very dark, brownish in the mass, the sign of extreme concentration. The mouth is an extension of the nose, redolent of all the fruitiness of Pinot, the most delicate of all the grape varieties, a clear fruitiness melting into darker tertiary aromas. The alcohol-acid and tannin balance is perfect, a magnificent harmony, supple, powerful, almost velvety; the finale is as elegant is it is long.

Secrets of quality

Very great heat, small harvest, balanced concentration.

Availability

Practically impossible to find.

Current price

Not on the market.

Apogee
1950, but still extraordinary.

Comparable or almost comparable vintages: 1928 1929, 1937.

development: appears to be unchanging. Should be drunk before it is a century old.

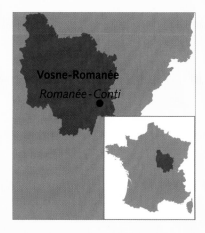

Tradition

Wine drunk by the Prince de Conti was made in exactly the same way as the 1921 vintage. It came from the same vines, planted in the same place, in a vineyard of the same size. The yield per hectare may have been smaller in the eighteenth century than it was in 1921, though in that year the harvest was very small and the yield in the property is severely limited to between 25 and 30 hectoliters per hectare.

Château d'Yquem 1921 Bordeaux – Sauternes

Château d'Yquem is a ruined twelfth century fortress of which only a few walls remain. Shortly before the French Revolution, Count Louis-Amédée de Lur-Saluces married Joséphine Sauvage, whose ancestors had acquired Yquem in 1592. Since that time, the Lur-Saluces family worked tirelessly to pursue constant perfection for this incomparable château-bottled wine. However, in March, 1999 Château d'Yquem was bought by the French luxury products group LVMH.

The vineyard is huge, a single stretch of 113 hectares, planted with 80% Sémillon and 20% Sauvignon (seven thousand plants per hectare). The siliceous Graves soil is poor. It has been improved by human intervention since in the time of Charles X (nineteenth century), the Lur-Saluces have buried 100 kilometers of drainage pipes in the soil! The grape-pickers pass along each row of vines several times, so as to pick only those attacked by botrytis (the Noble Rot.) The grapes are said to be "rôties" (roasted). The grapes are then lightly trodden and pressed gently several times. The must then ferments directly in casks until the degree of alcohol reaches about 14-15°, when fermentation stops spontaneously. Aging in new casks lasts for three and a half years. The wine is drawn off several times and it is clarified twice with bentonite. It is then filtered a final time before being bottled. Atmospheric conditions do not always favor noble rot in which case for that year there is no Château d'Yquem at all. This is what happened in 1951, 1952, 1964, 1972, 1974, and 1994, in the post-war years alone. On the other hand 1921 was the year in which everything combined to make it Yquem of the century.

Following pages:
Old wines from
Château d'Yquem.

Organoleptic Description

Today, the robe of Château d'Yquem 1921 is dark mahogany. A heady mixture of aromas of citrus and plum, honey, vanilla-scented candied apricots precede the basic creamy, smooth, subtle texture and a mouth as long as it is harmonious. It is an ageless masterpiece because it develops without turning rancid.

Secrets of quality

Maturity, concentration and botrytisation.

Availability

Rare... but not impossible to find.

Current price

FF 7,500
(1,143 euros).

Apogee
1950 ?

Comparable, or almost comparable vintages: 1967, 1988, 1990.

Development:
to be drunk before it is 100 years old.

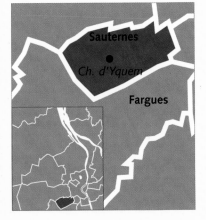

Weather Conditions

In the spring, a sharp frost attacked the vine as it was sprouting. A lot of heat was then needed to obtain the perfect ripening and hoped-for concentration.upon maturity. In 1921, conditions were just right. After the usual mid-August storm, the fine weather returned and continued until the fall, without being affected by the morning mists rising from the Garonne and the Ciron.

The vines had never been watered so little, hence the unparalleled richness and concentration of the grape juice. The pickers began work on September 13, and spent 39 days in the vineyard, passing along each row five times. The ideal balance of 14-15° of alcohol, plus six degrees of potential alcohol (120 grams of sugar per liter) was easily obtained.

1

2

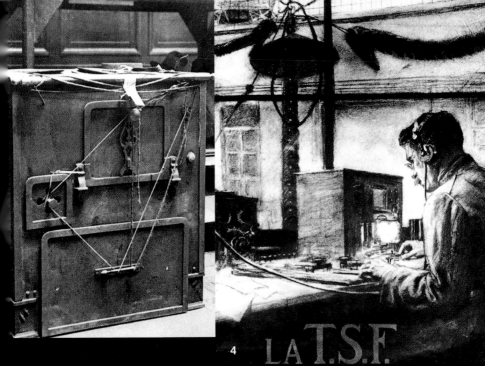

LA T.S.F.

4

5

. Germany in crisis
After World War I, unemployment
and deflation caused the German
economy to slump to its lowest level.

. Racing circuits
In the 1920s, automobile races attracted
large and enthusiastic crowds.

. The Landru trial
The French Bluebeard was sent to the
guillotine in 1922 for strangling and burning
11 people, ten of them women, in this huge
iron oven.

. Wireless telegraphy
This invention made it possible to transmit
messages simultaneously to the four corners
of the earth.

. Walt Disney
Walt Disney, producer, director, and animator,
releases his first film.

1928

From today's perspective, the most important event is the accidental discovery of penicillin by Alexander Fleming. But there was a more immediate and apparent milestone when telephone lines linking Paris to New York or Algiers were inaugurated. Television sets were manufactured by the new production line techniques and offered to New Yorkers at reasonable prices, although the clarity of the images left a lot to be desired, since they were composed of between 28 and 48 lines (the American system now uses 625 lines). Von Opel's car could get up to a speed of 200 km an hour (125 m.p.h) in his *"fusauto"* (rocket automobile) and aeronautical applications were being considered. In politics, extremism becomes the order of the day. Pope Pius XI had "excommunicated" the right-wing Action Française two years earlier; the French Communist Party engages in class warfare, the Nazis are elected to power in Bavaria. Chiang Kai-Shek becomes president of the Republic of China, whose seat of government is located in Nanking.

The French dominate world tennis and the Roland-Garros stadium, a rival to Wimbledon and Forest Hills opens. Sport begins to arouse overenthusiasm. Thirty spectators are injured after a soccer match played between France and Belgium.

Facing page:
Dovecote on
the Château Latour
estate.

Mickey Mouse is born. Musical hits include George Gershwin's *An American in Paris* in New York, Bertolt Brecht 's *Threepenny Opera* in Berlin, and Maurice Ravel's *Bolero*.

Château Latour 1928 Bordeaux – Pauillac

In 1928, the masters of Château Latour could claim to be celebrating more than two hundred and fifty years of ownership of the estate but they could not have known that they were about to vinify the greatest red wine ever produced—though Romanée-Conti comes a close second. At the beginning of this book, the 1928-1929 pair of vintage years was mentioned, the rigorous construction of the 1928s and the magnificent fruitiness of the 1929s, in both the Bordeaux district and Burgundy. We stated that it was logical to compare the wines side by side, glass by glass, as wines at their respective apogee. To be able to make such a comparison the wines had to reach their respective peaks at the same time. It might have been expected that two successive vintages would come together at their best, but this did not happen. The 1929, despite starting a year later, made up for lost time, and blossomed in a brilliant firework; and as it went out with a bang, the *"colossal"* 1928 vintage began its inevitable rise. Thus when the younger wine had generally passed its best, the older wine was only just getting there.

The yields per hectare of these two vintages were normal (about eighty barrels). The harvesting weather was magnificent and both vintages sold at the same price, 20,000 French Francs a barrel, a record at the time.

Following pages:
harvesting basket.

Organoleptic Description

Terribly tannic, with a high alcohol content, and incredibly concentrated, Château Latour 1928 is a legendary wine. Even today, it needs to be heavily oxygenated (by decanting it into a carafe) in order for it to be seen in its best light. Even after all these years, the robe is deep pomegranate color and has hardly developed at all. The complex, spicy bouquet with tertiary aromas of licorice and leather, heralds a mouth with a tight warp and weft, in which the tannins are clearly present but eventually melt and concentrate in an exemplary manner which is indefinitely prolonged into a harmonious finale.

Secrets of quality
Very small grapes and exceptional ripeness.

Availability
Fetches high prices at auction.

Current price
FF 3,500 (534 euros).

Apogee
2000 (magnum).

Comparable, or almost comparable, vintages:
1945, 1961.

Development:
Drinkable until its 100th birthday.

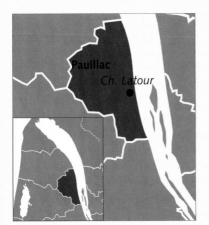

Weather Conditions

There is no doubt that for thirty years or so, the Latour 1929 was the best wine, but since then the Latour 1928 has overtaken it.
How is it possible for the two wines to be so different? The summer was slightly hotter in 1928 than in 1929, there were more grapes to the bunch but they were smaller and their skin was very tough. That is due to an excess of heat and lack of rain, whereas in 1929 a few showers "humanized" the grape.

Salon 1928 Champagne

The harvest began on September 24, perfect bunches of grapes being harvested, and the must reached the crucial level of 10 to 12° of alcohol. The acidity was considerable, in the order of seven or eight grams a liter, an indicator of quality. The serious drought in August caused the growers to predict a limited harvest but they had not taken into account the cool, damp nights and early morning dew of September. The bunches of grapes were numerous and weighed about two hundred grams (7 ounces) each, twice as much as usual. At the time, the volume of the harvest was judged to be satisfactory (six thousand kilos per hectare). It would not be considered very good today, when yields that are twice as big are customary.

Aimé Salon was a self-made man, a hard worker but great sybarite. He was a hard worker because he had started with nothing and made his fortune. The term "sybarite" also fits him perfectly because he kept a table open at *Maxim's*, so that his friends could dine at his expense, even if he were not there. As one of the richest men in France, he had developed a taste for the good life. He had an immoderate love of champagne and had two chefs at his disposal. His sister had married a cellar-master from Mesnil-sur-Oger, which gave him a taste for Chardonnay and he discovered a passion for the wines of Mesnil-sur-Oger. He bought a few vines and had some champagne produced for his own use and that of his friends. Not knowing the constraints he fixed his own rules of production and decided that his champagne should be made exclusively from white grapes. At the time, *Blanc de Blanc*, now so fashionable, did not exist. He decided to use only

The 1928
vintage in the Salon
cellar.

grapes from the commune of Mesnil-sur-Oger and only to make
champagne in the good years, thus champagne that would always be
vintage. Needless to say, only the first pressing, the *cuvée*, was good enough
to make this exceptional champagne. These four rules still govern the
making of Salon champagne. It was so heavily in demand by those who
wanted to drink it that Aimé Salon eventually sold his champagne on the
open market. The first vintage dates was the 1911. It subsequently became
Maxim's "official" champagne.

Aimé Salon died in 1943, and was succeeded by his sister, who bequeathed
the firm to her grandson, Marcel Guillaume.

Nine years later, problems of joint ownership forced Marcel Guillaume
to sell Salon. Dubonnet-Cinzano, then Pernod-Ricard, and finally
Laurent-Perrier became the successive owners, but none of them altered
the strange operating methods. Where the money comes to operate the
estate does not matter if those who run the firm are unshakeable in their
resolve as was the case with Robert Billon until his death.

Again, the author begs the reader's indulgence for bringing himself into the story because he knew those involved and was a neighbor of Marcel Guillaume until his death. Guillaume drank champagne, morning, noon, and night, and always in tall glasses, to show that there was nothing special about this habit which was merely part of everyday life.

From Aimé Salon, he had not only inherited the champagne-producing firm but also a love of good food. He loved to cook and created dishes using the tricks he had learned from his uncle, of whom he spoke such a lot that I ended up by feeling I had met him myself. Robert Billon lived in an attractive modern house that directly faced the Clos du Mesnil (which now belongs to Krug). He ran the firm and operated a small grape-purchasing cooperative, reserved exclusively for the wine-makers of Mesnil-sur-Oger. Marcel Guillaume had thought up this system in order to be certain of the provenance of grapes destined to be used to make Salon champagne.

Robert Billon was what some people would call "macho," others would call

Aimé Salon,
founder of the
firm in the early
twentieth century.

him a philanderer. One day, he came home and his wife, who had reached the end of her tether, was waiting for him with knife in her hand. She stabbed him in the stomach, killing him instantly.

Going down into the Salon cellars with him was a memorable experience. It was also a dangerous one, because there has never been such a damp cellar and more slippery steps. Water did not ooze from the walls, it literally poured out. Robert Billon would withdraw the 1928 "hoard" from a narrow cleft, and this would be the first bottle we would drink. It had to be tasted immediately uncorking (cork-oak was used of course because crown caps for wine were unknown at the time). A masterpiece!

At the time of writing, Didier Depond runs Salon. It is owned by Laurent-Perrier, that is to say Bernard de Nonencourt. He has taken over Salon champagne and Delamotte champagne—two adjoining firms. Delamotte belonged to his brother, Charles de Nonencourt, who had married Marcel Guillaume's sister!

The world of Champagne is quite a closed one, as this story shows.

Organoleptic Description

The golden color of the robe is faded, but the gas is still there, the tiny bubbles constantly moving the liquid around. The nose is rather that of buttered hazelnut than almond and there is complete absence of maderisation. The lemony aroma is rounded. The words "candied" or "crystallized" are not appropriate because the wine is too lively for that. There may be a hint of honey but without the heaviness this could imply. In the mouth there is a complexity and vigorous finesse. And what length in the mouth! A very great white wine.

Secrets of quality
Magnificent summer weather and cold nights.

Availability
Extremely rare.

Current price
Not on the market.

Apogee
Around 1945.

Comparable or almost comparable vintage:
possibly 1996?

Development:
drink as long as the cork keeps the gas inside.

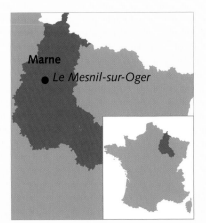

Weather Conditions

That year, the whole of France experienced the same weather conditions, a hot, dry August followed by a September of the same type. In Champagne, there were frosts as late as May and in some places hail had fallen in June and damaged the vines. The clincher was the September weather, when nights and mornings were very cool. Experience shows that strongly contrasting temperatures at that time of year are likely to produce great vintages.

1

2

1. Tennis
Heroes of the French tennis team: Borotra, Brugnon, Cochet, and Lacoste, the golden age of French male players.

2. Republic of China
Chiang Kai-Shek becomes president.

3. Al Capone
In the United States, Prohibition (1919-1933) produces smugglers, bootleggers et speakeasies—and, of course, the Mafia and organized crime.

4. The Roaring Twenties
Evening on the Champs-Élysées, in Paris in the late 1920s.

5. Traffic
Parisians discover the joys of traffic jams.

1929

The sensation of the year was unquestionably New York's Wall Street Crash which occurred on Thursday October 24. Stocks lost one third of their value, causing some speculators to commit suicide. The day was known as "Black Thursday." Italy finally sorted out its problem with the Vatican, which became a sovereign state as a result of the Lateran Pact. In Geneva, the writer Aristide Briand launched a plan for a United States of Europe; in Jerusalem, Jews and Arabs fought at the foot of the Wailing Wall. Automobile races were all the rage; Monaco organized its first Grand Prix, which was won by Williams driving a Bugatti. A "gentleman driver" who also won acclaim for finishing brilliantly in a Bugatti was Philippe de Rothschild, owner and dynamic manager of château mouton rothschild, a Superior Growth from Médoc and one of the greatest wines of France. Shortly thereafter, he came second behind Chiron at the Grand Prix des Nations at Neubergring in Germany. Both were driving Bugattis, beating the Mercedes on their own ground.

The era of mergers had already begun, however. General Motors bought Opel from Carl Benz (born in 1844). Benz had built the first gasoline-fueled vehicle and "self-propelled" himself on a motorized tricycle on July 3, 1886. Several leading Frenchmen died in that year, notably Georges Clemenceau, Marshal Foch, Georges Courteline, and Antoine Bourdelle.

Facing page:
château de
la Mission
Haut-Brion.

1929

Part two

Château la Mission Haut-Brion 1929
Bordeaux – Pessac-Léognan

From 1630 to the French Revolution, this estate belonged to the clergy. It then passed through three or four hands until 1920, when it was acquired by Frédéric Woltner. This innovator and perfectionist was the first to try vinification in metal vats (in 1926) and understood the need to check and regulate the fermentation temperature.

The sublime 1929 vintage was the result of this technical progress. In 1983, the "Woltner estates" (Mission Haut-Brion, Latour Haut-Brion, and Laville Haut-Brion) were incorporated into Clarence Dillon SA, a corporation based at Haut-Brion. Today, the vineyard covers about 21 hectares of günzian gravel soil planted with 60% of Cabernet Sauvignon, 30% Merlot and 5% Cabernet Franc. The vines are old and the yield is low, only about 35 hectoliters per hectare. Today, the winestore is all stainless steel and computerization, the cutting edge of wine technology. Frédéric Woltner had just as modern an outlook in 1926, but vinification and grape cultivation techniques have hardly changed since 1929. Fermentation is at 30°C and aging is in new hogsheads. Although 1929 is later than 1928 the more recent wine should be drunk earlier. Château la Mission Haut-Brion is a delightful claret, devoid of mischief or superficiality, and richly elegant. Some vintages are great in their excess, but this is not the case with the 1929 which is all harmony, the supreme expression of balance. The Château de la Mission Haut-Brion 1929 exemplifies the epitome of the qualities required for a great vintage, an unforgettable composition of unsurpassed harmony.

Organoleptic Description

A wonderful robe, as is frequently the case with Mission, complex, abundant and varied fruitiness, followed by a mouthfeel which is a combination of sugar-plums and puréed mulberries, highlighted by a hint of licorice and pitch. All this, with the roundness of an old Banyuls. An unparalleled harmony.

Secrets of quality
The grapes and perfect vinification.

Availability
Rare.

Current price
FF 1,700 (259 euros).

Apogee
1950.

Comparable or almost comparable vintages: 1949, 1955, 1956, 1961.

Development: still good to drink.

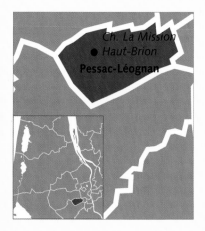

Ch. La Mission
● Haut-Brion
Pessac-Léognan

Weather Conditions

The previous year, 1928, had been very hot and dry, almost excessively so. The year 1929 was similar, but with a series of perfect seasons. Growers were hoping for rain, and when the rain fell, it was in reasonable amounts, just enough to "encourage" the harvest without drowning it. It should be remarked in passing that the last such "double"—two great years in succession—1899-1900, was followed by three disastrous ones. That is exactly what happened after 1928-1929, when there were three poor years.

1. Vatican

As a result of the Lateran Agreements, signed by Cardinal Gaspari on behalf of the Holy See and Mussolini on behalf of Italy, the Vatican becomes a sovereign state subject only to the authority of the Pope.

2. The Wall Street Crash

Wall Street on Thursday, October 24: the stock market crashes and this day becomes known in history as Black Thursday. It was the first, but by no means the last, great crisis of international capitalism.

3. Georges Clemenceau

Death of the great French writer and statesman, defender of Dreyfus.

4. Automobile Races

The first Monaco Grand Prix.

5. *Marius* staged in the theater

This four-act play is the last in the "Marseille Trilogy" (the others are *Fanny* and *César)* by Marcel Pagnol.

1934

A turbulent year of violence and assassination. France is still reeling from the Stavisky Affair in France which ended in the death, presumed to be suicide, of the shady financier in December, 1933. In Paris, rioting against political corruption claims several victims. In Marseilles, King Alexander I of Yugoslavia, the former crown prince of Serbia, is shot dead by a member of the Ustashi, the pro-Nazi Croatian terrorist movement, who also kills the French foreign minister, Louis Barthou. In Germany, Hitler uses his SS to organize the Night of the Long Knives to rid himself of his staunch supporter, Ernst Röhm and the SA (brownshirts). The death of Chancellor Hindenburg opens the way for Hitler to declare himself Chancellor of the Reich, and combining this with the presidency the Nazis assassinate the Austrian chancellor, Dollfuss. In Spain, two provinces demand independence and the young Spanish Republic is threatened with civil war. War breaks out in China. Chiang Kai-Shek's army defeats Mao Zedong's Communists who begin their Long March. The very popular Albert I, king of the Belgians, is killed in an accident. His son, Leopold III, succeeds him on the throne. France, under the right-wing Laval tries appeasement with Italy and signs a non-aggression treaty over Africa. Other non-aggression treaties are signed between Germany and Poland, and the Soviet Union and Poland, and a pact is entered into between Yugoslavia, Greece, Romania, and Turkey.

Facing page:
Austrian vineyard in
the Rust region.

The Labour Party wins its first election in Great Britain and in France, Marcel Cachin, a Communist, sets up a left-wing alliance, the Popular Front.

Ruster Ausbruch 1934
Austrian wine – Neusiedlersee-Hügelland

The name is hard to translate. *Ruster* indicates that the wine comes from the village of Rust in the Burgenland district of Austria. As for *Ausbruch*, it may be derived from the word *Aszü*, a wine made from withered grapes or those rotted by *Botrytis cinerea*, but this would not be absolutely accurate because the words *Ausbruch* and *Aszü* also have a technical meaning and both indicate a specific method of wine-making. This will be explained later in greater depth.

Ruster Ausbruch is not as famous a wine as, say, Château Lafite or Clos de Vougeot, but a wine from Rust won a medal at the Vinexpo in 1985 and a Ruster Ausbruch won the International Trophy for Sweet Wines in London in 1995.

Grapes have been grown in Rust for a long time. There are records of wine-making here and in neighboring villages dating from 1317 and it is even possible that Charlemagne introduced Burgundy vine stocks into Burgenland in the late eighth century. In the Middle Ages, the wines of Rust were designated "wines of the emperors" because the Hapsburgs drank them. The honor is an interesting one because it shows that the reputation of the vines of the region precedes the making of sweet wines. There has always been a dispute between Austria and Hungary as to which was the first to make fine wines. It should be remembered that Burgenland has only been Austrian since 1921 ; prior to that date, it belonged to Hungary and the present frontier is very near Rust. This explains the presence of the Furmint grape, which is well known in the Tokay region. In fact, Rust and Tokay vie with the honor of being the first to make wines

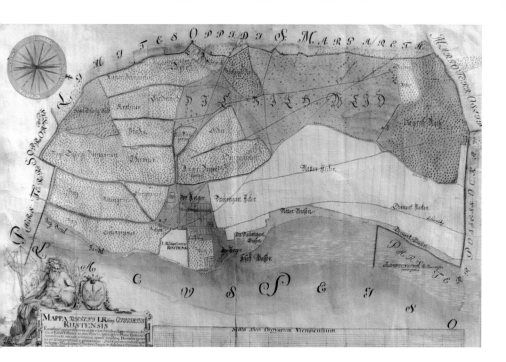

Mappa Terreni Civitatis Rustensis, map of the Rust vineyard, 1783.

from grapes attacked by the "noble rot." However, according to a chronicle which was published in Venice, Italy in 1441, the first such wine came from Moldavia (currently in Romania) and was called Cotnari, a sweet white wine which gained international renown in the nineteenth century and is still made today.

To return to the chronology, in 1526 a wine made from the juice of "rotten grapes" is mentioned in the village of Donnerskirchen, a few miles to the northeast of Rust. The tax ledger of the village of Weiden records that from October 16 through November 13, 1617, moldy grapes were harvested which yielded 357 hectoliters of Ausbruch.

All of these wines were made from Furmint grapes attacked by botrytis, as was the earliest Tokay that has been traced, vinified in 1631 by the reformist minister Maté Szepsi Leczko, from grapes harvested in the Oremus vineyard. The fact that Leczko was a reformist minister is not surprising because the Lutherans encouraged the vinification of rotten grapes, being unaware or deliberately flouting the prohibition on this grape, judged to be "impure" by the Catholics (after all, these wines were intended for use in the Mass). The Protestants were the traveling salesmen of the botrytised grapes.

If the technique of making wine from rotten grapes had emerged in Rust and the neighboring villages of Donnerskirchen and Weiden it is because this is the European heartland of Botrytis. The fungus mold, *Botrytis cinerea*, proliferates here because the natural conditions are ideal for its growth. All these villages lie close to a very large expanse of water that covers several dozen square miles. The Neusiedlersee is the largest lake in Central Europe and it is very shallow, being no more than two meters (6 feet 6 inches) at its deepest point. This means that, despite the semi-continental climate of extremes, there is a thick morning mist produced by evaporation of the Neusiedlersee, as much as 225 million hectoliters annually!

Harvesting is performed either by the *trie* method, picking only the rotten grapes and returning several times as in the Sauternes district, or as in Hungary by using two buckets and sorting as they are picked, or by cutting out the moldy grapes. *Ausbruch* comes from the German word *ausgebrochen*, "cut out." Ausbruch is the result of a special vinification

process. The botrytised grapes pass through a pre-fermentation phase, then a must that is not so rich is added to them, which reactivates fermentation. The result is a wine that is richer in alcohol but less rich in sugar. An Ausbruch is balanced when it has 13° of alcohol and 150 grams of sugar. A Trockenbeerenauslese has 9° of alcohol and 220 grams of sugar. Tokay Aszü *(see page 346)* is an inverted Ausbruch. The grapes affected by noble rot are incorporated into the basic wine; the quantity of botritysed grape berries is expressed in *puttonyos*. A *puttonyo* is a wooden tub which can hold around 35 liters of the grapes.

Friedrich Seiler, present owner of the estate.

The balance of a dessert wine is not expressed entirely in terms of the sugar-alcohol ratio, it also needs a lot of acidity. In the Rust region, the wines are rich in tartaric acid. Then there is the aging process. The problem is the same at Tokay as in Rust. The extended, oxidizing aging process is disappearing since the result is unpopular with modern consumers. That is why pre-war Ausbruchs are so different from those of today, though it is impossible to compare them with pre-war Tokay, since none are left.

Organoleptic Description

A rare bottle of 1934 Ruster Ausbruch was found and drunk in 1973. The robe was mahogany-colored, and the wine was distinguished by the complex elegance of the bouquet, the lively and delicate balance and by the very long length in the mouth. The discernible oxidation of the wine was clearly the result of old-style vinification methods rather than of aging, since the longevity of the Ausbruchs is exemplary. The wine is extremely rich—it can attain 25° of alcohol—and is made from Welsch Riesling (a very sweet grape rich in tartaric acid). There is a fruitiness with a hint of burnt toast and the oxidation of the aging technique marries well with the creamy complexity of the noble rot. This memorable Ruster Ausbruch is very different from the livelier and fresher wines that have been vinified since World War II and especially since 1990.

Secret of quality
Perfect mastery of the noble rot technique.

Availability
None, not even in Austria.

Current price
Not on the market.

Apogee
1960.

Comparable or almost comparable vintages:
1963, 1981 ;
contemporary style: 1993.

Development: long past its prime.

Rust
Neusiedlersee-Hügelland

Weather Conditions
Wine-makers remember the year 1934, as the one when the noble rot was at its most vigorous, striking with amazing speed. It attacked the overripe grapes the result of the hot, dry summer which caused the early harvest (starting September 2).

1. Murder in Marseilles
King Alexander I of Yugoslavia, traveling through France, and the French foreign minister, Louis Barthou, were both assassinated by Pétrus Kalemen, a member of the Croatian right-wing terrorist organization called the Ustashi.

2. The Long March
In 1934, Mao Zedong's army began its Long March, that did not end until 1936.

3. Rioting in Paris
Violent demonstrations and confrontations between the police and the Communists left 12 dead and hundreds of wounded.

4. Pierre and Marie Curie
Death of Marie Walewska Curie, winner of the Nobel Prize for Physics in 1903 and for Chemistry in 1911.

5. Hitler and Mussolini
The rise of Nazism and Fascism in Europe.

1935

The hit song of the year in France is the strangely prophetic *Tout va très bien, madame la marquise* (Everything's Going Swell, Milady), performed by Ray Ventura and his orchestra, while Italy and Germany were defying the rest of the world.

Germany was busy breaking the Treaty of Versailles, and rearming to the hilt, reintroducing military service, and promulgating legislation to exclude Jews from normal daily life. Italy invades Abyssinia (Ethiopia) heedless of the sanctions against it voted in by the League of Nations. The Soviet Union invented the "stakhanovite," a word taken from the name of a model miner who broke all the productivity records. A stakhanovite becomes the word for a "work hero," a model, and privileged Soviet citizen in receipt of a higher salary and extra privileges. Work begins on building the *Normandie* the French flagship ocean liner. Paris holds its first Concours d'Élégance in which luxury cars are displayed along with models dressed in the latest haute couture fashions. Queen Astrid of Belgium is killed in a car accident while being driven by the king, causing a wave of grief to sweep through the country. Paul Signac, the painter who made Saint-Tropez famous, dies, as do André Citroën and T. E. Lawrence (Lawrence of Arabia) who is killed in a motorcycle accident. This is also the year of the death of the French writers Paul Bourget and Henri Barbusse, the Portuguese poet Fernando Pessoa, and the composer Alban Berg.

Facing:
Frank "Smiler"
Fladgate *(right),* a
director of Taylor
from 1897 through
1950.

Taylor Vintage 1935 Portuguese – port wine

In Bordeaux, 1935 was a year which is never mentioned.In Burgundy, it
does not have much of a reputation. The summer was not unpleasant
but the rains came early in the fall. The wines were not very
concentrated although the ripeness was acceptable. Not a single French
appellation produced a memorable wine, but the story was very
different in Portugal.

It is interesting to note that it is often the case that a great year for
Portugal wines is often a poor one for the rest of Europe and vice versa.
Thus, 1928 and 1929 were merely average in Portugal whereas 1927
and 1931 were praiseworthy. The situation was reversed on the French
side of the Pyrénées (and the same applies to 1960 and 1963, great
Portuguese vintages, miserable results elsewhere).

Port is not always given a vintage (like champagne) and its vinification,
blending, and aging are very special because it is not bottled until it has
spent two years in a pipe or cask, tawny ports remaining in the wood
for even longer. The two types of port can easily be distinguished by
sight because as tawny oxidizes in the wood, it turns a reddish color
(hence the name), while vintage ports remain very dark because they
are protected from oxidation by being held captive in the bottle.

Taylor is a very old, traditional firm, founded in 1692 by the English, of
course, like most of the great traditional port wine producers. The vintage
ports have the distinction of aging very slowly, to such an extent that the
experts consider that they need to spend 15 years in the bottle for them to
mature properly and reveal their typical aromas.

Organoleptic Description

The robe of this 1935 vintage port is starting to show its age at the edge of the disk. It is thick and oozes down the glass. To the nose, this heady, characteristic richness which is far from heavy is characteristic of vintage ports. There is an alliance of brutality and grace, a complex fruitiness approaching but never being overwhelmed by oxidation. Once this first difficulty has been overcome, the art is to put virility into the sweet roundness of the mouth. In this 1935, this is achieved memorably. The result is immense harmony, finesse, and length in the mouth. It is the quintessence of a valuable vintage port.

Secrets of quality
Perfect maturity, limited yield.

Availability
Only at English auctions.

Current price
Unknown.

Apogee
1985.

Comparable or almost comparable vintages:
1945, 1963.

Development:
should be drunk before 2010.

Weather Conditions

The summer of 1935 was warm and dry in the Douro, ideal conditions for maturity and superb harvests. The volume was average and the grapes were harvested at the usual time, the last week in September. Considering the conditions, it is not surprising that a number of *quintas* decided to make a vintage port.

1. **The** *Normandie*
The steamer, on its first crossing of the
Atlantic, welcomes New Yorkers on board for
the return trip.

2. **Antisemitism in the East**
The SA and the SS force Jews to pick up
garbage and clean the streets of Vienna.

3. **Louis Lumière**
French inventory of cinematography with one
of his projection machines.

4. **Stakhanovism**
Construction of a turbo-generator in
Leningrad.

5. **Fred Perry, tennis star of the 1930s**
In 1934, the English tennis star won the
Davis Cup for the second time for his team
and won the French championship.

1937

The Civil War breaks out in Spain while Japan invades China.
Guernica is bombed by the Germans and Generalissimo Franco leads
the Phalange, the sole political party Italy bans marriage between
Blacks and Whites in its colonies and slams the door on the League
of Nations, becoming the ally of Japan and Germany in an
anti-Komintern pact.

In Great Britain, George VI is crowned in December 1936, his brother
Edward VIII (who became the Duke of Windsor) having abdicated
in his favor, in order to marry the American divorcee, Wallis Simpson.
In France, the French national railways SNCF (Société nationale des
chemins de fer français) is created and the Universal Exposition is
at its height. The *Normandie* winsthe Blue Ribband for the fastest crossing
between Europe and the United States. The German dirigeable,
Hindenburg, explodes upon arrival in New York, causing the death
of a hundred people. Travel by airship is banned. In the United States,
Henry Ford introduces a 32-hour week into his factories. Du Pont in
Nemours, Belgium, patents a new type of fiber called Nylon.

The world of music lost Maurice Ravel, George Gershwin,
and the blues singer Bessie Smith. The Baron de Coubertin, who
revived the modern Olympic Games, also died. In Italy,
the Communist theoretician Antonio Gramsci and the physicist Marconi,
inventor of radio, breathed their last.

Facing page :
a vintage bottle of
La Tâche.

La Tâche 1937 Burgundy

It might be considered surprising that the year 1937 could be the best year for a red wine. It is well known that this was a great year for whites, in the Bordeaux district (dry and dessert wines, the Château d'Yquem 1937, is still as full and majestic as ever) as well as in the Loire where the best of the oldest vintages were harvested in 1928, 1937, and 1947. One had to have tasted a sparkling Vouvray 1937 by Huet or the 1937 Château Moncontour to discover that a champagne never offered such delicate and complex aromas of tea and linden blossom as the old Chenins were capable of producing. The year 1937 was also a great one in Champagne, Alsace, and Germany where the hocks made from Riesling grapes had not produced anything as great since 1921. So why La Tâche? Because in that year, the red Burgundies were unparalleled, and there is no question that these were the greatest red wines of the century.

The faintness of the acidity, which is typical of the 1937 vintage, improved the white wines and incorporated itself ideally into the red Burgundies. They still had a hint of vigor, a touch which would have affected the balance of a claret but in this case simply enhanced and developed the fruitiness of the Pinot grapes.

And why La Tâche 1937? It is a rare wine in all senses. Rare, because so much of this excellent wine has been drunk, hardly any is left; rare, because war interfered with its normal distribution; rare, finally, because it combines components that are often contradictory.

Organoleptic Description

The robe is dark, typically of this vineyard which is generous in the color of its wines. Its density is repeated in the mouth. There is a certain paradox between this roundness and the fresh, vigor, a tone above what one might expect. The bouquet is flamboyant and rich, so typical of the grape variety that it could be a wine used for teaching. It seems to be saying: "This is what Pinot is all about!" The fruitiness of the Pinot resists tertiary aromas, but there is a hint of smokiness nevertheless. The finale, is very rich and lasts for a long time. Some bottles seem to be unsurpassable.

Secrets of quality

Fine weather with cool evenings.

Availability

Extremely rare.

Current price

None available but a figure of FF 4,000 (610 euros) would seem reasonable.

Apogee
1975?

Comparable or almost comparable vintages:
1921, 1929.

Development: its vigor and richness have been maintained but it ought to be drunk as soon as possible.

Vosne-Romanée

La Tâche

Weather Conditions

While average summer temperature in the Bordeaux district was mild, the sun shone brightly in Burgundy from July through September. Harvesting began in late September in optimum conditions—the grapes were healthy and ripe.

1. Coronation of King George VI

After the abdication of Edward VIII, who chose to marry twice-divorced Wallis Simpson, George VI is crowned king of England.

2. Civil War in Spain

Guernica is bombed and a bloody Civil War engulfs the country.

3. Invention of Nylon

Du Pont of Nemours, Belgium starts making Nylon fabric.

4. French railways and paid vacations

French vacationers leaving from the Gare d'Orsay in 1936 on their first paid summer vacation.

5. The *Hindenburg*

Upon arrival in New York at the end of its twenty-first voyage, the German dirigeable explodes, causing the death of a hundred people.

1945

1945

The War is over at last, and Europe celebrates the Liberation. Although it has an army of five million men, Japan is on the verge of capitulation. General de Gaulle takes over the French government and nationalizes the banks, Air France, and Renault. Social security becomes compulsory and French women are finally granted the vote. The Communist win the elections in France and there is a Labour landslide in Great Britain. Churchill resigns and Clement Attlee becomes prime minister. In the United States, Roosevelt dies in office and Harry Truman takes over. The American, British, and Soviets organize the conferences of Yalta and Potsdam. Eastern Europe is handed to the Soviet Union. In Palestine, the clashes between Jews and Arabs become more frequent and both attack the British to attempt to hasten their departure (they rule the country under a Mandate from the League of Nations). The Jews demand a national homeland.

Ho Chi Minh proclaims the Democratic Republic of Vietnam. The consequences of the war are not long in coming. The trials of the Nazi war criminals open at Nuremberg. In France, the collaborationist ruler, Marshal Pétain, is condemned to death but is interned in the fortress of Portalet. In the space of two days, Hitler commits suicide and Mussolini is executed. The United Nations and UNESCO will be created in the following year. On the cultural level, the French poet, Paul Valéry and the Hungarian musician,

Facing page:
Mouton Rothschild
1945.

Béla Bartók die. The first post-war Nobel Prize for medicine is awarded to Alexander Fleming for the discovery of antibiotics.

CHÂTEAU

... LA RÉCOLTE M... ...

1945

Cette récolte

...boums numérotés

magnums numér. de...

...teut & ½ bout. numér

Réserve du Château m...

...bouteille porte le N°...

a produit
de A à U
M 1 à M 175
de 1 à 74422
marquées R.C.
56,802
...ppe de Rothschild

ANNÉE DE LA VICTOIRE

MISE EN BOUTEILLES AU CHÂTEAU

Château Mouton Rothschild 1945

Bordeaux – Pauillac

Never, unless it was in 1893, which could be considered as "the" vintage year of the nineteenth century, had flowering been so early. Under such conditions, it is no surprise to learn that harvesting began at the end of the first week in September. Nor should it be a surprise to learn that the yield per hectare was the lowest it had been for fifty or sixty years (in the order of 10 h per ha). This record was beaten, however, in 1961 when the harvest was even smaller. Not only were there few grapes to a bunch but they were very small. The juice was greatly concentrated and the ratio between skin area and volume was extremely favorable to maximum extraction. Furthermore, the grapes were completely ripe, the richness of the musts sometimes attaining 15° of potential alcohol!

Other factors contributed to making the first post-war harvest an exceptional and rare one and these were due to the War itself. For one thing, the vineyard was not replanted, so the average age of the vines was high. Nor had they been fertilized for several years. In any case, since 1750 at least, wine-makers know that fertilizer and quality do not go together.

So the raw material was ideal; now it was up to the vinification, without removal of the stalks and without the modern cooling methods. As might be expected, the best vinification is performed by the cellar-masters of the *grands crus*, the great estates who for more than two centuries have devoted the greatest care to creating fine wines. All of the Bordeaux Premiers Crus are exceptional which can be considered the greatest of the great? Latour is often mentioned, but Mouton even more often.The label, the first of a series which still continues, was the work of Philippe Julian.

Following pages:
Baron Philippe
de Rothschild,
owner of Mouton
Rothschild and racing
car enthusiast.

Organoleptic Description

The robe of this legendary wine has remained dark and opaque, though there is an imperceptible browning at the edge of the disk. The bouquet is typical of "flamboyant mouton"—baroque, spicy, luxuriant, almost uncontrolled. After this, the body appears to be disciplined, but it is there, unfailingly. There is a balance between the alcohol (significant), acidity (important), and tannin (very concentrated) which appears to be "standard" though in fact it is much more than that an archetypal mouton, an archetypal 1945.

Secrets of quality

Early flowering, great concentration and richness of the musts (very low yields), total maturity, excellent grape quality, highly skilled vinification.

Apogee
Around 1985?

Comparable or almost comparable vintages: 1961, 1949, then 1947.

Availability

The star attraction of numerous wine auctions.

development:
to be drunk preferably before 2020.

Current price

FF 12,100
(1,845 euros).

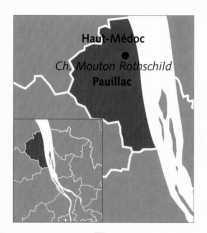

Haut-Médoc
Ch. Mouton Rothschild
Pauillac

Weather Conditions

The fact that this was the first post-war harvest ought to have been enough to immortalize the vintage, but the freak weather conditions made it even more memorable. In the first few days of May, there was a sudden, heavy, and very late frost, which blackened four-fifths of the vineyard. The Merlot vines, which flower earlier than the Cabernets, were the worst affected. Subsequent hot, dry weather soon restored the situation, but the harvest was extremely small.

Clos des Lambrays 1945 Burgundy

A historic, miraculous enclosed vineyard. There is evidence of Clos des Lambrays in the fourteenth century. The vineyard took its name from a Burgundian family that was very promi-nent in the Middle Ages. All trace of it was subsequently lost and it disappeared after the French Revolution, when estates were broken up as a result of inheritances. Then along came an extraordinary man named Louis Joly who decided to buck the trend. He embarked on an amazing reconstruction, buying 75 plots of land, one by one, and managed to reconstitute the Clos des Lambrays to make it into a "monopole"

Facing page:
wine-cellar at
the Clos.

(where all the wine of one type is made from the grapes on the estate). Or rather, almost a "monopole" because 420 m² eluded him, and that is the reason why about two hundred bottles of Clos des Lambrays are labeled with the name of Jean Taupenot, wine-maker of Morey-Saint-Denis. Since 1988, the other thirty-five thousand bottles are the work of Albert-Sébastien Rodier and his descendants.

In 1938, Albert Rodier sold the Clos des Lambrays to Renée Cosson, a woman of great character who was passionate about sculpture and guarded her wine jealously. While her husband continued working as a banker in Paris, she lived in the seventeenth-century mansion overlooking a park planted with magnificent rare trees. She considered her wine to be a work of art, commercial considerations were of no interest to her. She wanted minute yields, so she let the vineyard age, because old vines "make good but little." She allowed her wine ferment for longer than anyone else's and left it to age in the wood indefinitely...

Such practices are dangerous and are not always successful, but if there is an element of luck, the resulting wine may be of exceptional quality. However, this attitude creates havoc in the modern world, where performance and profitability are the watchwords.

Renée Cosson had trouble with the authorities who refused to classify all the plots of land of which the Clos des Lambrays consists as a Grand Cru. This was totally unacceptable to her because the two sacred words "Grand Cru" were written on the labels of her bottles while the authorities, in the absence of an agreement, continued to classify them in the lower category of Premier Cru.

Madame Cosson died in the late 1970s, and she had gone too far in some respects but had made some interesting choices, as several of the vintages prove. The vineyard had become too old and contained several "manquants" (missing plants, dead vines), the fermentation vat was an antique and wines that were too old were still stagnating in the wood... The reserve of old vintages was impressive, however. Her son was unable to retain the property and the Saier brothers acquired it in 1979. The authorities classified 8,6618 hectares (out of 8,6975) as being Grand Cru and replanting began. In late 1996, a new proprietor took over, Günther Freud, a German national, acquired a totally new Clos des Lambrays.

Mansion and vine-
yard at the Clos
des Lambrays.

Organoleptic Description

A unique wine, the quintessence of this great soil. The robe is legendary, so lasting that it has no age, the spicy bouquet is unique to Clos des Lambrays, with its touch of bergamot and vanilla. The mouth is even more extraordinary, in its concentration, its syrupy, melting quality, its roundness and the mildness of the alcohol. Its supple smoothness is like that of no other wine. It can well be believed that neither at the Clos des Lambrays nor anywhere else will such a wine be made ever again.

Secrets of quality
Derisory yields, old vines.

Availability
Sometimes sold by specialist wine merchants.

Current price
FF 7,000 – FF 8,000 (1,067 – 1,220 euros).

Apogee
1975.

Comparable or almost comparable vintage: none, but 1937 and 1949 come close.

Development: still excellent to drink.

Weather Conditions

The year 1945 was the greatest for French wines. Early bad weather sharply reduced yields, and the sun did the rest later. The soil is low in potassium, a problem which later affected Burgundy would later suffer. The grapes were small, concentrated, perfect, especially at Clos des Lambrays with its very old vines. It is unlikely this set of circumstances will ever occur again.

1

2

4

5

1. The Liberation
Liberated Paris celebrates joyfully.

2. Votes for Women
French women are finally granted the right to vote, which they exercise for the first time in 1946.

3. André Gide
The publication of his *Journal*, which he began in 1943 was completed in 1953.

4. Atom bombs dropped on Hiroshima and Nagasaki
After the bombing of Hiroshima in August 6, a second atom bomb was exploded over Nagasaki on August 9. Japan surrendered.

5. Alexander Fleming
The British doctor discovered penicillin in 1928 and won the Nobel Prize for Medicine for the discovery of another antibiotic in 1945. He was appointed Rector of Edinburgh University in 1952.

1947

The aftermath of World War II hangs over Europe. France reorganizes slowly and painfully. Rationing of food and commodities continues. General de Gaulle resigns and the Fourth Republic is founded. The first president is the Socialist, Vincent Auriol, and the Socialist Paul Ramadier becomes President of the Council (prime minister).

In New York, the United Nations is preoccupied with the Palestine question, prelude to the creation of the State of Israel. The British intercept the *Exodus*, a ship containing four thousand Jewish refugees who intend to emigrate illegally to Palestine and send them back to Hamburg, Germany. Colonial empires founder, Nehru and Gandhi are instrumental in winning independence for India and Pakistan is created. There is rebellion in French Indochina. Communist dictatorships spread throughout eastern Europe. King Michael of Romania abdicates. The Iron Curtain is not yet closed but the Soviet Union is busy forging links in the chain mail. In Great Britain, Princess Elizabeth, the heir to the throne, marries Lieutenant Philip Mountbatten, who is made Duke of Edinburgh. The year 1947 is the year of nationalization and major strikes in industry in France and Italy. It also sees the beginnings of the workings of the Marshall Plan.

The Frenchman, André Gide, wins the Nobel Prize for Literature. While the world enters a new phase, nature is bestowing her exceptional bounty…

Facing page:
Château
Cheval Blanc, 1947.

1947

Château Cheval Blanc 1947
Bordeaux – Saint-Émilion

The estate consists of a single plot of land 37 hectares, east of the town of Saint-Émilion. Its gravel soil is planted with one third of Merlot vines and two-thirds Cabernet Franc vines (about 6,000 plants per hectare), a mixture which is unknown in other vineyards.

Château Cheval Blanc is the youngest of the Premiers Crus, since it has only existed since 1854. It remained in the family of the owner until fall, 1998.

Facing page:
Gaston Vaissière,
cellar-master at
the time of the
1947 vintage.

The climate which prevailed during the 1947 vintage can be summed up in one sentence: glorious weather from April 1 through the end of October, that is to say during the vegetative cycle. It was extremely hot (35 through 38°C [95-100°F]) and dry, and there restrictions were imposed on the use of water in the Bordeaux district.

When heat and dryness are excessive and persistent, the sap cannot play its part, the leaves wither and drop off the vine. Without leaves, without chlorophyll, the grapes themselves do not receive sugar. This phenomenon is known as growth blockage and is much feared by vine-growers in dry regions. It is a calamity that rarely occurs in the Bordeaux district, however, since the climate is almost always temperate due to the proximity of the Atlantic. If there is the sort of heat wave which occurs three or four times a century, there is almost certain to be a storm on August 15. But in 1947, the storm arrived a week late, on August 21 and when there was some rain in places in September, it did not fall until 19 and 20, when most of the grapes had been harvested. Under these conditions, it is not surprising that flowering was consistent

Organoleptic Description

The 1947 Château de Fesles is an unchanged and unchanging
wine, even though the robe contains mahogany tints. The bouquet

1

2

1. Establishment of the State of Israel
The United Nations studied the Palestine question as a prelude to the creation of the State of Israel, which would be established in 1948 by David Ben-Gourion.

2. Indian Independence
Negotiations between the British government and Indian leaders, attended by Nehru et Gandhi, resulted in the independence of India and the creation of Pakistan.

3. Albert Camus
The French author won the coveted Grand Prix des Critiques for his last novel, *The Plague.*

4. Automotive industry
Death of Henry Ford, founder of one of the largest automotive concerns in the world.

5. Royal marriage
Princess Elisabeth marries Lieutenant Philip Mountbatten, who becomes the Duke of Edinburgh.

1949

the situation worsens. France proclaims the independence of Vietnam. President Auriol signs an agreement with the former Emperor of Annam, Bao Dai, a controversial figure who returns to Vietnam after incorporating Cochin-China into the Vietnamese state. This is all that was needed to prompt the Viet-minh rebels to declare war on the French. Egypt still refuses to recognize the young State of Israel after invading it as soon as it was established, but signs an armistice with it. The proposal to internationalize Jerusalem continues to be a bone of contention for both Jews and Arabs.

War funds technological progress. An airplane breaks the sound barrier and flies at an altitude of more than 23,000 meters, the first passenger jet plane, the Comet, is built and goes into service in the United Kingdom and the first electronic calculator, invented three years earlier, is revealed to the world. There are rumors that IBM intends to manufacture and sell these machines. The great advance in medicine is the identification of the influenza virus. This makes vaccination a possibility. In France, there is an innovation in broadcasting whose impact is unforeseen. A journalist named Pierre Sabbagh presents a new type of broadcast, the television newsreel. Three broadcasts a week are planned. William Faulkner receives the Nobel Prize for Literature, and the literary world is shaken by the publication of the book entitled *1984*, by George Orwell, a politico-social work of science fiction written in 1948 (the author merely reversed the last two figures), about daily life under a totalitarian regime. George Orwell, a Socialist, denounces Stalinism; he was to die in January, 1950.

The composer Richard Strauss dies at the age of eighty-five; the French violinist, Ginette Neveu, is killed in a plane crash on a flight from Paris to New York which also claims the life of the former French boxing champion, Marcel Cerdan. In Belgium, two leading figures pass away, Maurice Maeterlinck, winner of the Nobel Prize for Literature, whose works include the libretto for *Pelléas et Mélisande*, Debussy's only opera, and James Ensor, a great painter whose work is in some way reminiscent of that of Hieronymus Bosch.

Opposite:
harvesting baskets.

Organoleptic Description

The 1949 Musigny de Vogüé 1949 is the epitome of everything that one could expect from the climate of the Musigny vintages. The robe is not the brightest but the most beautiful, the most elegant, the most joyful. As for the nose, the most elegant of the grape stocks also becomes the most harmonious. The famous little red grapes are there, with a flavor that is closer to rasperry than cherry, closer to blackcurrant than to mulberry, with a hint of licorice and spice. All these flavors can be found in the mouth which is silky, melting, crowned by miraculous well-integrated, subtle tannins. It is not a question of length in the mouth because the memory of such a wine does not disappear.

Secrets of quality

A very specific growing area, old vines, limited yield.

Availability

Sometimes sold at auction.

Current price

FF 2,100 (320 euros).

Apogee
1980.

Comparable or almost comparable vintages:
1959, 1945.

Development:
still perfect in a magnum, but should be drunk soon.

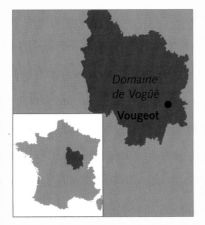

Weather Conditions

Much has been written on the respective merits of the years 1945, 1947, and 1949. In 1945, there was an extreme concentration of juice, in 1947, extreme heat, but in 1949 there was extreme classicism. In all three years, the grapes were healthy and ripe. The summers were record-breaking—long, hot, and dry. This dryness also caused five thousand hectares of forests to burn in the Landes, causing the death of nearly eighty people. In early September, a little rain saved the grape harvest. At the end of the month, perfect grapes were poured into the vats, a truly wonderful crop.

4

5

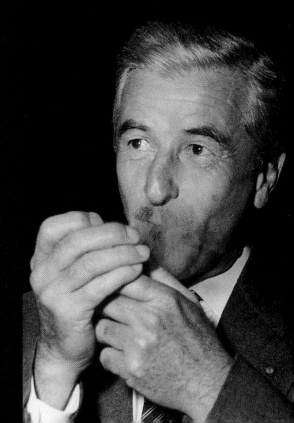

1. People's Republic of China
Mao Zedong proclaims the People's Republic of China after deposing Tchang Kaï-Shek, and reinforces his links with the Soviet Union.

2. Television
Birth of the television newsreel, presented by Pierre Sabbagh and broadcast three times a week.

3. Marcel Cerdan
The former world champion dies in a plane crash between Paris and New York.

4. Rita Hayworth
The American film star marries Prince Ali Khan.

5. William Faulkner
The American writer receives the Nobel Prize for Literature.

1959

President De Gaulle takes office, having been elected president of the French Republic in late December, 1958. He offers self-determination to Algeria.

In Cuba, Fidel Castro ousts the dictator, Fulgencio Batista, at the very end of 1958. He becomes prime minister and nationalizes land. The break with the United States is complete. The Belgian Congo is granted independence. The Dalai Lama, the spiritual leader, flees from his native Tibet, which is under the brutal domination of the Chinese; he takes up residence in India.

The space race between the Soviet Union and the United States continues to turn in favor of the Soviets who have a rocket-launcher that is infinitely more powerful than that of the Americans. The Soviet space probe *Lunik I* is the first object ever to escape from Earth's gravity. *Lunik II* reaches the moon, and *Lunik III* orbits the moon and transmits photos from the side that cannot be seen from Earth. The Americans send two monkeys into space. The Russians do the same with two dogs and a rabbit.

In the south of France, the Malpasset dam bursts and causes the death of more than four hundred people at Fréjus. The world celebrates the weddings of the Shah of Iran and Farah Diba and of Jacques Charrier and Brigitte Bardot. The economist and sociologist André Siegfried, dies and the world of music mourns the passing of the composer Heitor Villa-Lobos and the jazz musicians, Sidney Bechet, Eleanor "Billie" Holiday, and Lester Young. The French heart-throb Gérard Philippe also dies.

Opposite:
the circular
winestore at
Château
Lafite Rothschild.

Château Lafite Rothschild 1959
Bordeaux – Pauillac

This is a vintage which has always been referred to with the greatest respect, though in certain places, there has been a muttering of "it's too much, too much," said with downcast eyes as if the speaker wanted to be excused for his ungratefulness. Wines of this year achieved such an unusually high sugar content, that special dispensations were granted to Champagnes whose degree of alcohol exceeded what was permitted under the rules of the appellation !

The acidity level was low, closer to that of 1947 than to 1951, yet strangely, the wines are not heavy or flat, which might happen in the circumstances.

With its hundred hectares, Lafite is the largest of the Premier Cru estates. It has a long history which intermingles with that of the *parlement* (council of nobles) of Bordeaux. Between the seventeenth century and the present, two famous names are connected with the estate, Ségur and Rothschild. The counts of Ségur made the wine's reputation and cossetted the vines for more than a century. James de Rothschild acquired the vineyard when it was auctioned off in 1868. He paid about FF 4,400,000 for it, a record price at the time.

The vineyard has remained in the Rothschild family ever since.

In 1959, the deep gravel soil of Lafite played its important part in ensuring that the vine was able to withstand the extremely hot summer without wilting. The result is a very great wine, no doubt the first among first of the year, though Lafite has often enjoyed the title of Premier des Premiers.

Organoleptic Description

The robe shows a certain development but the hue remains dark; the revelation comes when one sniffs a glass. The most subtle aromas of this Lafite approach those of cedar, emphasized here by a fruitiness of candied mulberries and cookies. In the mouth, the cedar turns to licorice and vanilla, smooth and dark. The richness of the 1959 harvest gave this wine an elegant but strong structure, melting and harmonious, an indication of its longevity.

Secret of quality
Soil that is drought-resistant.

Availability
Sometimes sold at auction.

Current price
FF 1,750 (267 euros).

Apogee
1985.

Comparable or almost comparable vintages:
1945, 1961.

Development:
to be drunk before 2010
(the largest sized bottles will keep better but must be laid down with care).

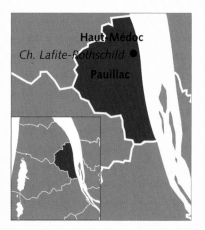

Weather Conditions

There was a near-disaster because July and August—July more than August—were months of drought, which caused a blockage in vegetation in the Bordeaux district, though rain fell in the end. In Burgundy, harvesting began in dry weather from the second half of September. It was one week later in Bordeaux.

1. Kruschev and Eisenhower
Detente between the great powers with the first visit to the United States of a Soviet head of state. The two presidents met to discuss the problem of Germany and its disarmament.

2. Royal wedding
The Shah of Iran marries Farah Diba.

3. Fidel Castro
Violent demonstrations in favor of the Cuban leader force the dictator Batista out of office. He flees to the Dominican Republic. Fidel Castro becomes head of state.

4. De Gaulle President of France
General de Gaulle takes up residence in the Élysée Palace, having been elected president of the French Republic in late December, 1958.

5. Marriage of the stars
Brigitte Bardot marries Jacques Charrier.

1 9 6 1

1961

Man goes into outer space for the first time. On April 12, the Soviet cosmonaut, Yuri Gagarin orbits the earth on board the *Vostok I*. The American response is swift; on May 5, Alan Shepard takes up the challenge on board the *Mercury III*. The Berlin Wall is erected by the East Germans, thereby preventing escape to the West. Hassan II becomes king of Morocco. Trouble erupts again in the former Belgian Congo, when there is pressure for the copper-rich province of Katanga to break away under Patrice Lumumba, former Congolese prime minister. Lumumba is arrested and assassinated by the head of the Congolese army, General Mobutu. The UN blue berets are sent in to restore order. In Algiers, four French generals hatch a plot to keep Algeria French. Meanwhile, a conference is held in Evian, France, between the French government and the Algerian nationalists. Meanwhile, General Salan, ringleader of the French rebel soldiers, takes over the loyalist OAS, created to keep Algeria French. There is an abortive attempt to assassinate de Gaulle.

In Israel, Adolf Eichmann is tried for masterminding the deportation of millions of Jews. He is condemned to death.

The British protectorate ends in Kuwait and the Iraqis make the first of many attempts to claim the oil-rich state as a province. The Bay of Pigs incident,

Facing page: cellar of the Paul Jaboulet Aîné estate.

an American attempt to assist anti-castro Cubans to invade Cuba, ends in a standoff, thanks to Soviet threats. The writers, Blaise Cendrars, Céline, and Ernest Hemingway die as does the psychoanalyst Carl Gustav Jung.

Hermitage la Chapelle 1961 Rhône

In 1961, the weather follows the same pattern throughout France. There is bright sunshine throughout the whole summer and for a good part of the fall. On the other hand, the spring weather is varied, but despite this the results are very similar, in the Bordeaux district and in the Rhône Valley. In the Bordeaux district, there is a sharp frost which breaks into a spell of fine spring weather, drastically reducing the yield (a qualitative factor). In the Rhône Valley, the spring is very wet, causing severe wilt of the buds, again ensuring that the volume is small.

The vineyards of Paul Jaboulet Aîné see their average production of 40 hl per ha fall to 15 hl per ha. Syrah grapes (the only variety used to produce red Hermitage) are harvested on the only hill on the estate. "La Chapelle" is a brand name, as opposed to the name of a particular vineyard or plot of land. The grapes come from five hectares in the Bessards and sixteen hectares in the Méals; the normal yield is a hundred thousand bottles (though not in 1961).

Nowadays, the harvest is sorted and the stalks discarded but this was not the case in 1961. The vinification is not particularly unusual (fermentation at less than 30°C (86°F) for about ten days, and *remontage* [see Glossary] for three hours a day) but the aging process required the wine to be aged in casks of oak from the Jura, which produced more mellow tannins than those of the Allier oak. The wine is bottled without being filtered but being lightly clarified with bentonite.

Following pages:
view of the estate.

Organoleptic Description

The 1961 Hermitage la Chapelle 1961 is inky black and almost unaffected by age. The fruitiness is explosive, concentrated, and complex. There is a density that is also found in the mouth with the mellow scent of sugarplums. The tertiary aromas are of high quality, smelling of balsam with hints of tar. This mellow, fruity concentration is reminiscent of the port wine aromas of the 1947 Château Cheval Blanc. The wine is extreme and complete.

Secret of quality

The concentration.

Availability

Scarce.

Current price

FF 2,300 (351 euros).

Apogee
1990.

Comparable or almost comparable vintages: 1929, 1978, 1983.

Development: to be drunk preferably before it is fifty years old.

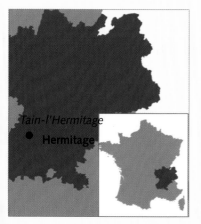

Tain-l'Hermitage
● Hermitage

Weather Conditions

There was a sharp frost in the spring, interrupting a spell of good weather, drastically reducing production in the Bordeaux region. In the Rhône Valley the bad weather came in the form of rain, causing the young shoots to dampen off, guaranteeing a meager harvest.

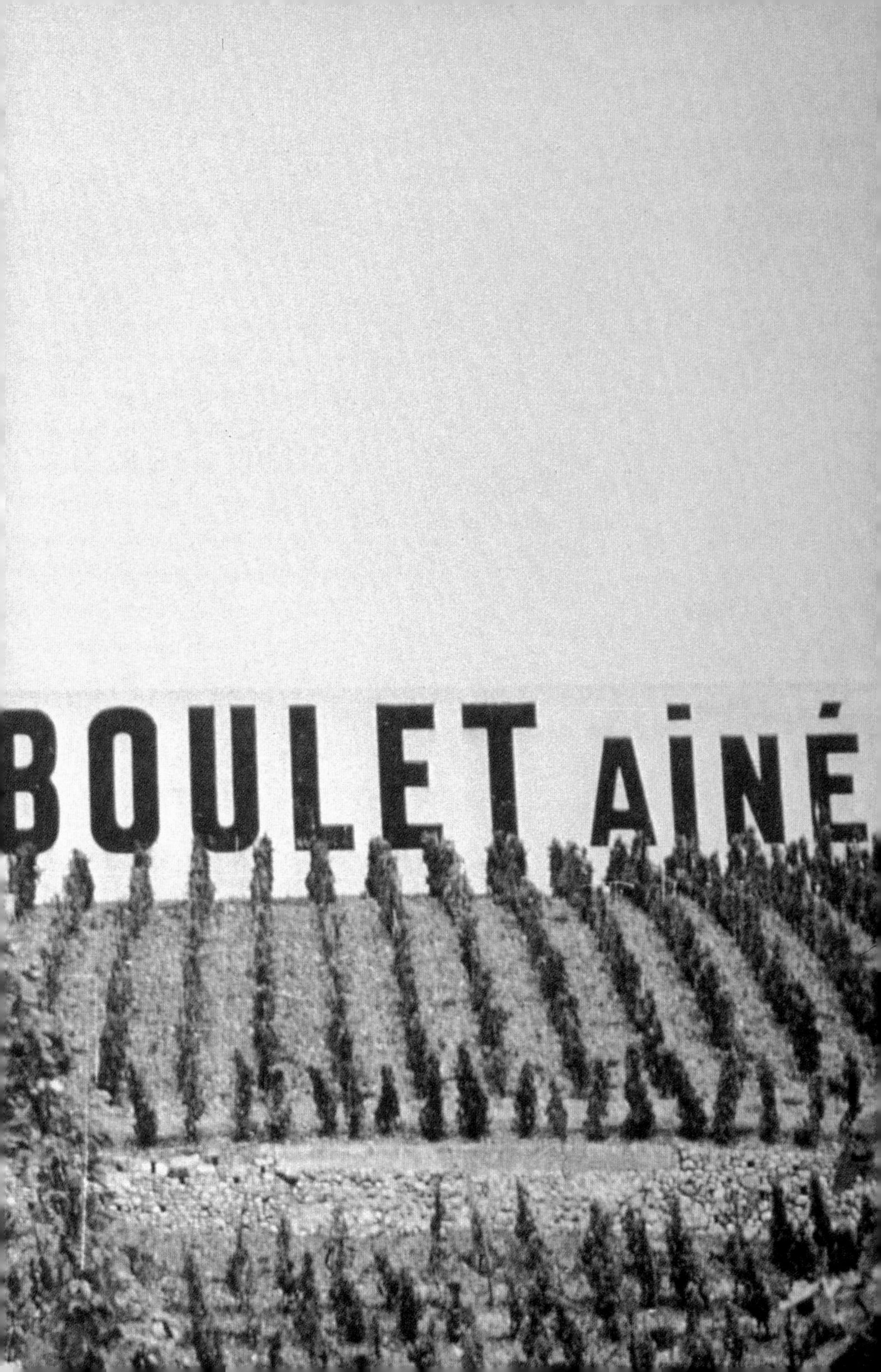
BOULET AiNÉ

Château Latour 1961 Bordeaux – Pauillac

The vintage was exemplary and is often quoted as "the"vintage of the century. Although the phrase tends to be over-used, this Château Latour can at least claim to be the vintage of the half-century.

Everything happened that year as if nature had decided to have all the luck on her side, with the dual purpose of seriously reducing the yield, while obtaining perfect maturity and an ideal harvest.

That is exactly what happened.

There was a warm spell early in the year but it was followed by a late frost which damaged the vines. This was not the first time for such a weather pattern; frost always reduces the yield and hot summers ensure that the grape ripens perfectly.

Facing page:
the 1961 vintage.

The vintages of 1945 and 1961 are comparable, in that they were two record years of very small yields amounting to 10 and 8 hectoliters per hectare respectively.

At Latour, the harvest began on 16 September but lasted only ten days, due to the poor quality of the grape. The grapes were small, almost dried out.

Under such conditions, the volume produced was barely a third more than the normal harvest (63 barrels were produced in 1961 as against 166 in 1960).

In that year, some Bordeaux wine-makers wanted to delay the harvest until October, not to overripen the grapes, which was not desirable, but no doubt hoping for providential rains which might perhaps increase the size of the few grapes that remained on the vine. This was in vain,

because even then the rains failed to come. Finally, morale was saved because the grapes might be of a better quality, even if the quantity was greatly diminished.

Everyone knew that the vintage would be exceptional if the excessively rich musts and the warmth of the grapes harvested did not cause fermentation to be prematurely arrested, something which is always to be feared under these conditions. A high degree of alcohol was to be expected, as well as very ripe tannins and an extraction rate. There might also have been too low a level of acidity, causing the wine to be flat and too long. None of this happened. The concentration and richness of the must could only lead to the production of one of the great wines suitable for keeping over a long period.

The vintage has not disappointed; the wines may have reached their apogee a few years ago but they remain excellent.

Of all the 1961 vintages, Latour has had the slowest development. It barely reached the peak of perfection when all the other great wines of the century had long passed theirs.

Courtyard of the winestore.

Organoleptic Description

The robe is extremely dark and dense, while the weft and warp of the bouquet is so tight that it gives the impression of opacity. It is an extract of spices which is almost introverted.
In the mouth, the wine imposes its stature and concentration, one could almost call it a "square roundness." It is full, spherical, but also straight, taught, and the finale is as harmonious as it is powerful, as complex as it is long.

Secrets of quality
Maturity and low yield.

Apogee
2000.

Availability
The star of the French wine auctions.

Comparable or almost comparable vintages:
1928, 1945.

Current price
FF 3,200 (488 euros).

Development:
should be drunk before 2025.

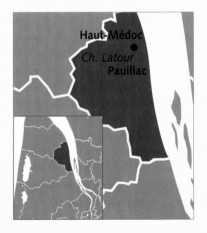

Weather Conditions

It was unusually warm at the beginning of the year, so the vines sprouted early. Then three frosts, between 17 and 29 March, blackened and killed off the shoots. Sunny weather in May hastened flowering but at the very moment of pollination, there was another cold spell which caused the flowers to wilt. The harvest was bound to be very small. End of act one. The second act opened more traditionally with magnificent hot weather and harvesting in the sun. Yet despite all that has been written about it, the summer and heat of 1961 were not record-breaking; at least seven or eight were hotter, though it was one of the hottest of the twentieth century. The temperature was not that high, but on a few afternoons it exceeded 40°C (104°F)! This concentrated the grape juice. The almost total absence of rain (except on September 20) and the burning south wind further dried the grapes.

1. The Berlin Wall
The construction of a concrete wall fencing off East Berlin stopped the East Germans fleeing to the West.

2. Coup d'Etat in Algiers
Three of the four French generals. (From left to right: Zeller, Jouhaud, and Salan) who were responsible for the Algiers putsch which caused worldwide consternation. They were condemned by de Gaulle.

3. Ernest Hemingway
Death of the American writer who won the Nobel Prize for Literature in 1954.

4. John and Jackie Kennedy
The first Roman Catholic president of the United States took office in January, 1961.

5. The Conquest of Space
Yuri Gagarin, immediately prior to takeoff in the *Vostok* spaceship, when he became the first man in space.

1962

The war in Algeria ends. With the Évian agreements, Ben Bella becomes the first head of government of the independent Algeria. The exodus of the "pieds-noirs," the French colonists, begins. The OAS sees the end of its dream of a French Algeria. There is another attempt on the life of General de Gaulle and again he escapes. He holds a referendum on the direct election of a president of the French Republic by a 60% vote. War is narrowly avoided between the Soviets and the Americans when Khrushchev installs missile launchers in Cuba, and Kennedy threatens to sink and bomb Russian ships carrying the missiles. The Soviet ships turn back. But in space, the Soviets increase their lead. The Americans put an astronaut, Lieutenant-colonel John Glenn briefly into orbit (three trips round the earth), the Soviets orbit the earth almost fifty times in *Vostok II* and *IV*. The United States consoles itself with *Mariner*, the probe that passes three hundred kilometers from Venus and transmits photographs of the planet. The Pope excommunicates Fidel Castro. The ocean liner *France* is launched and the tunnel under Mont-Blanc is completed. A pop group from Liverpool make a recording at Decca Records, which the company eventually fails to release because it doubts that it will be any good. The group is called the Beatles. John Steinbeck wins the Nobel Prize for Literature. Marilyn Monroe dies under suspicious circumstances. The painter Yves Klein dies prematurely. The world of literature loses Bachelard, Nimier, Faulkner, and Hesse.

Facing page:
Penfolds Grange
Hermitage 1962.

enfolds

Max Schubert

ge Hermitage

BIN 95

1961 <u>BOTTLED</u> 1962

Penfolds Grange 1962 Australian wine

A change of hemisphere means a change of world. This wine comes from Australia a country where the grapes are harvested in March or April. Although the change of seasons is an oddity to which one soon acclimatizes, the "change of world" is very obvious in the viticulture which is very different to anything that happens in the Old World.

The way that the Spanish *bodegas* is vaguely reminiscent of Australian customs, but only vaguely because the *bodegas* of the Rioja, for example, procure their grapes only in the Rioja and thus produce a wine labeled Rioja (which has its own appellation). In Australia, although growing areas, regions, and sub-regions have recently been established, the concept of estate-bottling and vineyards, as they are understood in Europe, does not exist. Grapes from distant reasons can thus be combined and chosen exclusively on the basis of the properties, or their compatibility. Furthermore, Australia is in the forefront of modern technology and has exported *winemakers* (œnologists) all over the world. It is completely unaffected by European prejudices against irrigation or the use of harvesting machines. Penfolds is named for its creator, Dr. Christopher Rawson Penfold, who settled in Magill, near Adelaide, in the foothills of Mount Lofty, in 1844. This eccentric Englishman, who was a doctor, set himself up as a vine-grower and wine-maker, and was the first to introduce the grape variety known in Australia as Shiraz and in France as Syrah into the southern hemisphere. At the time his home was known as the "Hermitage of Grange Cottage," which is why his wine is known as Grange Hermitage. It is now known simply as "Grange" to distinguish it from the well-known French "hermitage,"

The winestores.

AOC, which is only made from one grape variety the Syrah. It is no accident that the red wines have a similar name. Max Schubert, who ran the operation starting in 1950, decided to create a great wine following a study trip to Bordeaux. However, he used a completely original approach, since he did not select a few outstanding plots of land, as would happen in Europe, but blended the best grapes, or the varieties that appeared to be the most compatible, to create a masterpiece.

The Shiraz grape, which is perfectly adapted to the clay and siliceous soil of the hills of Adelaide, the Morphett Vale, and the Barossa Valley, was the basis for the high quality wine. Pragmatic and unhindered by any formal training, Schubert discovered, adapted, and invented. The Australian vineyards began growing a large number of varieties but Cabernet Sauvignon was meeting with growing success. Schubert thus conceived the idea of blending Cabernet Sauvignon with Syrah in varying proportions, always with more of the Syrah. The Grange thus became a blended wine, like claret. The vinification, which is perfect of course, adheres to the following principles: complete removal of stalks (*éraflage*) extraction by submerging the cap (*chapeau*) at unusually low temperatures (in the order of 20° to 25°C (68-77°F) and aging in American oak barrels for about two years, followed by storage in bottles for four years. Like all pioneers and innovators, Max Schubert was faced with mounting criticism, until his wine won a gold medal at a major event in Sydney, in 1962, when it was pronounced the best wine in Australia. Not only did Penfolds Grange become the most expensive wine in Australia, but also one of the most expensive in the world, achieving prices somewhere between the Premiers and Second Crus Classés of Bordeaux. It is the only wine of its quality that does not come from a precisely defined location. Max Schubert managed to retain identical quality by constantly changing the composition of his blends, eliminating certain grapes, such as those from Morphett Vale (a vineyard which fell into the hands of developers) and replacing them with some from Clare Valley (200 kilometers away, but grapes from vineyards at a distance of 500 kilometers and more have been used).

Even though Penfolds Grange does not come from a specific plot of land, it

"He never leaves any

PENFOLD'S!

is nevertheless the product of very carefully selected grapes which certain derive their quality from the land on which they were grown. We are once again back with the indisputable merit of the concept of the land, but in a manner which Europeans would find it hard to accept. because it assumes that it is possible to conceive of a wine that would be made from, for example, a blend of Lafite, Cheval Blanc, and Hermitage. In fact, this is not as silly as it sounds because it is known that in the nineteenth century, the makers of Bordeaux "hermitaged" their wines.

Penfolds advertise-
ment of the late
19th century.

Organoleptic Description

The robe is very dark and dense, turning brown at the edge of the disk. The tertiary aromas of Syrah are mixed with exotic, spicy, vanilla-scented bouquets, to which are added mild notes of licorice, some of which are contributed by the American oak hogsheads. In the mouth, there is balance, full and fleshy, almost syrupy, roundness power and length in the mouth. This is a glory that has never been surpassed (production of about 80,000 bottles a year).

Secret of quality

Low yield (twenty to thirty hectoliters).

Availability

Sold at auction in Australia and possibly in the United Kingdom.

Current price

No transactions in France.

Apogee
Around 1976.

Comparable or almost comparable vintages:
1970, 1976.

Development:
to be drunk as soon as possible.

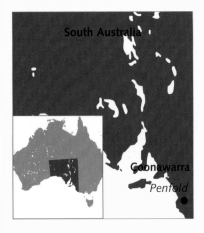

South Australia

Coonawarra

Penfold

A classic wine?

Is Penfolds Grange a classic wine? Not according to leading French œnologist Professor Peynaud. During a French television broadcast, the famous English œnophile, Jancis Robinson, author of best-selling books on wine, brought a bottle of Penfolds Grange Hermitage into the studio. Professor Peynaud smelled the bouquet and described it as "pharmaceutical," a term describing a category of aromas. Peynaud had never said such a thing about a Bordeaux which is normal, of course, because Penfolds does not try to imitate claret. Something to be said in its favor, when one considers how many imitators are around.

Penfolds
Grange Hermit
Penfolds
Grange Hermit
Penfolds
Grange Hermit

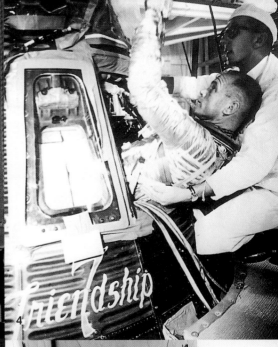

1. The Cold War
Aerial view of a Soviet warship taking its missiles back to the USSR at the end of the Cuban missile crisis. The United States had informed the USSR that it must remove its arms stationed in Cuba. Khrushchev agreed in exchange for an American undertaking not to invade Cuba.

2. End of the Algerian War
Exodus of the French colonists (known as *pieds noirs*) to Marseilles, after signature of the Évian agreements.

3. Marilyn Monroe
Death of the American star under circumstances that have never been fully explained.

4. Conquest of Space
Lieutenant-colonel John Glenn orbited the earth three times on board the *Mercury*, making him the second man in space after Yuri Gagarin.

5. The *France*
Launch of the transatlantic liner, s.s. *France*.

1964

1964 was the year in which the Beatles triumphed, the year of the miniskirt and the year when the Vatican came out firmly against the contraceptive pill. It was also a year of transition and commitment to the future. It was decided to build a tunnel under the English Channel, the American forces, (present in Vietnam as "advisors") are attacked by the North Vietnamese. Gamal Abd al-Nasser and Nikolai Khrushchev together inaugurate the Aswan High Dam. By the end of the year, Khrushchev would be replaced by Kosygin. A certain Brezhnev becomes head of the party. China explodes its first atom bomb. There is a surprising example of cooperation for the period between the Soviets and the Americans when they decide to cooperate to produce a satellite. The American rocket *Ranger 7* takes 4,316 photographs in space before crashing onto the moon.The United Kingdom abolishes the death penalty. Soccer once again claims many lives when 320 fans are killed after a football match in Lima, Peru. Jean-Paul Sartre rejects the Nobel Prize for Literature which is awarded to him.

Martin Luther King, Jr., is awarded the Nobel Peace Prize in recognition of his non-violent fight for Black civil rights. Nevertheless, three civil rights workers are murdered in Mississippi. The killers escape justice. Two leading politicians die, Jawarhalal Nehru, who had been prime minister of India since its independence, and Maurice Thorez, chairman of the French Communist Party.

Facing page:
Cellar of La Tenuta
Greppo ;
old bottles of
Brunello
di Montalcino.

Brunello di Montalcino 1964 Italian wine

To comprehend just how extraordinary Ferruccio Biondi-Santi's methods were in the years 1870 through 1880, one needs to remember what the wine scene was like in Italy at the time.

Today, every wine-growing country is in search of the best soil and climatic conditions for vine-growing and the aim is produce the best quality wine, so that the best practices are quite "normal." This was not at all the case 130 years ago in Italy. Despite the fact that Italy is the cradle of European viticulture and twenty centuries ago it was producing such legendary wines as Falernian, for fifteen hundred years it had languished into the production of "plonk," and although cheap wine has its uses it is no excuse for allowing the great wines to disappear. In the late nineteenth century, Ferruccio Biondi-Santi, owner of a vineyard in the little village of Montalcino, in Tuscany, eighty kilometers south of Sienna, took it into his head one day to select a particular variety of Sangiovese, the most popular vine stock in the region and the main ingredient in Chianti.

He eventually chose the smaller of the Sangiovese Grosso variety, giving it the name of Brunello. He propagated it in his vineyard and began to produce very distinctive wine. All that he did was completely against the traditions of Italian wine-making. He vinified a wine which had excellent keeping qualities, which required very long aging and was not worth drinking until many years of aging in the bottle. This was done in a country where wines had no aging qualities whatsoever.

In this context, Ferruccio Biondi-Santi's methods would seem to be

Harvest at
La Tenuta.

positively suicidal from a commercial point of view. And yet, as can be seen more than a century later, he was on the right track. It was not until the 1970s that Italian viticulture once again invested in a quest for great wines. When this happened, Brunello di Montalcino quite naturally become one of the first to benefit from a DOC, and then a DOCG, that is to say an appellation. The distinctive wine had been produced since the late nineteenth century by the same family, and was appreciated by connoisseurs throughout the world. Very sought after and the most expensive wine in Italy, it took its place among the great vintages of the world. There is no doubt that the initiative of the Biondi-Santi family was responsible for the production of the first of the great Italian wines. The Biondi-Santi family are still at the helm, although a lawyer has bought a share in the family business. The archives of the estate, which are preserved in the winestore, are extraordinary. The great registers are surprising in their modernity and provide a detailed description of all the vintages produced since 1880, with a detailed chemical analysis of each wine described. Brunello di Montalcino is certainly the only appellation of all the vintages, since the first, that has been described so precisely.

1 9 6 4

To introduce a wine that had been invented from scratch, the Biondi-Santi family had stuck to the most rigorous rules of production. They grew only Sangiovese Grosso, which has a low yield per hectare, and aged it in the wood for many years—four years for the Annata, five for the Riserva, the latter being made from old vines. Their rigor did not end there, because only the outstanding vintages had the right to be labeled Brunello di Montalcino Biondi-Santi, which meant rejecting the resulting wines for three years out of ten!

The estate.

Organoleptic Description

In 1964, Tancredi Biondi-Santi had the honor of vinifying the best ever Brunello di Montalcino, a wine of an exceptional caliber, whose pomegranate-colored robe had barely developed, with a bouquet of complex tertiary aromas which include violet and a hint of spices. The mouth remains strongly tannic (the presence of the tannins is emphasized by a slight acidity). All this combines into a rare fullness.
It is a wine which curiously combines sumptuousness, virility, and elegance.

Secrets of quality
Highly skilled vinification and perfect climatic conditions.

Availability
Rare (the estate has a well-stocked cellar; some of the bottles date back to 1890).

Current price
Few transactions.

Apogee
1990.

Comparable or almost comparable vintages: 1985, 1953, 1961.

Development:
preferably to be drunk before 2020.

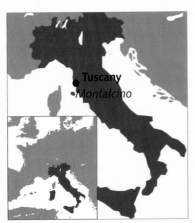

The Biondi-Santi Vineyard
15 hectares in the commune of Montalcino, south of Sienna
Grape variety: Sangiovese Grosso.
Production: 500 hl a year of Brunello di Montalcino.
Aging: 4 or 5 years (riserva) in the wood.
Alcohol content: 12.5° minimum.
Total acidity: 5.5‰.

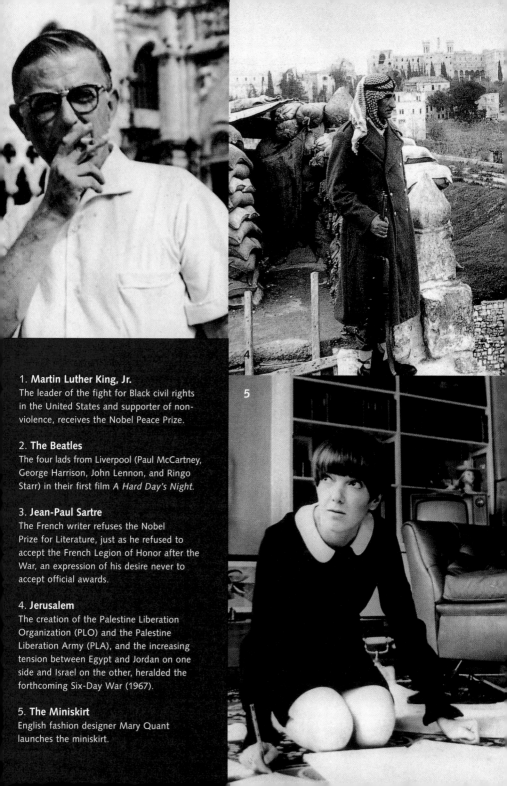

1. Martin Luther King, Jr.
The leader of the fight for Black civil rights in the United States and supporter of non-violence, receives the Nobel Peace Prize.

2. The Beatles
The four lads from Liverpool (Paul McCartney, George Harrison, John Lennon, and Ringo Starr) in their first film *A Hard Day's Night*.

3. Jean-Paul Sartre
The French writer refuses the Nobel Prize for Literature, just as he refused to accept the French Legion of Honor after the War, an expression of his desire never to accept official awards.

4. Jerusalem
The creation of the Palestine Liberation Organization (PLO) and the Palestine Liberation Army (PLA), and the increasing tension between Egypt and Jordan on one side and Israel on the other, heralded the forthcoming Six-Day War (1967).

5. The Miniskirt
English fashion designer Mary Quant launches the miniskirt.

1967

On a political level, this is a year of crisis. Che Guevara is killed in Bolivia; Régis Debray, his French sidekick, is arrested in Bolivia and sentenced to a term of 30 years imprisonment (he is released and expelled three years later). In Greece, the right-wing regime of the colonels takes over and the King Constantine is sent into exile. The Vietnam war intensifies. Another war, is over quickly but has lasting consequences. The Six-Day War is won resoundingly by Israel. Stalin's daughter, asks for asylum in the United States. General de Gaulle visits Quebec and, encouraged by an enthusiastic crowd, shouts "*Vive le Québec libre !*" (Long live free Quebec).
A mechanical digger is placed on the moon by *Surveyor III*, to dig out some rock. France, the United Kingdom, and Germany together design and build the *Airbus*. Dr Christian Barnaard, a South African surgeon, performs the first successful heart transplant operation, but the patient dies a month later from a pulmonary infection. The giant oil tanker, *Torrey Canyon*, founders, seriously polluting the English and Breton coastlines.
French television broadcasts in color for the first time.
Former German Chancellor Konrad Adenauer, architect with de Gaulle of Franco-German reconciliation, dies as do two other politicians, the French Marshal Juin and Clement Attlee, the first post-war prime minister. Robert Oppenheimer, who invented the atom bomb, also dies. The arts lose the painter René Magritte and the writers André Maurois and Marcel Aymé.

Opposite: cellar of the Perrin estates.

234

Château de Beaucastel 1967

Rhône – Châteauneuf-du-Pape

The vineyard of the Château de Beaucastel covers eighty hectares. Trace
the estate can be found as early as 1549, but vines were not planted un
the late eighteenth century.

When the Perrin family took over the estate in the twentieth century,
Beaucastel really began to flourish. In three generations, Beaucastel was
raised to the first rank of producers of the Châteauneuf-du-Pape appella
wine, combining tradition with judicious innovation. The estate is typical
the type of soil where the grapes for this wine grow best. There are poli
pebbles deposited by the River Rhone in the Pliocene Era and from the
Miocene Era, the soil has retained a red clay with some sand content an
less easily discernible subsoil of gray mollasse. The estate is innovative in
red varieties it uses, combining equal proportions (30%) of Grenache an
Mourvèdre. This is an exemplary combination since Grenache is an
oxidating variety which compensates for the anti-oxidating power of the
Mourvèdre. The remaining 40% of the vineyard consists of the tradition
varieties grown locally and accepted by the appellation. It should be add
that the white varieties are also unusual, because they include a large
proportion of an unusual variety—Roussane (80%). This Châteauneuf-c
Pape estate is also innovative, even unique, in its system of vinification,
which briefly heat the must (especially for Grenache). The method was
invented to combat oxidases and limit the use of sulfur. On the other ha
traditional methods are preferred for aging, which takes place in 50 hl v
The wine is clarified with egg white before being bottled. The Château c
Beaucastel 1967 benefited from the perfection of the grapes that year.

Organoleptic Description

The robe is dense though not unaffected by the passage of time. There is a slight browning and the edge tends toward orange in color. The bouquet is extremely complex and conjures up a cornucopea of candied fruits and spices. The Orient and the Mediterranean combine and the strong tertiary aromas of tobacco and tar intervene.
These aromas are perceptible again in the mouth, enhanced by the mild, almost mellow, tannins that are supple and melting. An example of accomplished elegance.

Secrets of quality
Ideal blending, perfect grapes.

Availability
Very occasionally found in auctions.

Current price
From FF 300 to 400 (46 to 61 euros).

Apogee
1985.

Comparable or almost comparable vintages: 1970, 1978, 1990.

Development: the tannins do not dry out but it ought to be drunk fairly soon.

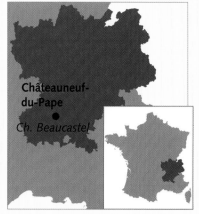

Châteauneuf-du-Pape

Ch. Beaucastel

Weather Conditions

It was an unlucky and disappointing year for most French wines, especially as hopes had been high as a result of good spring weather. Unfortunately, the fall ruined everything, the weather being so bad that in most places the grapes did not ripen properly, causing dilution. On average, the white wines did best. Alsace was spared the rains and produced excellent wines and the Sauternes survived them tthrough one of its famous Indian summers. Château d'Yquem vinified a legendary wine. The Rhône Valley managed to escape the fall rains and the grapes achieved ideal maturity, in a perfect state of health, with harvesters working in sunshine.

1

2

2

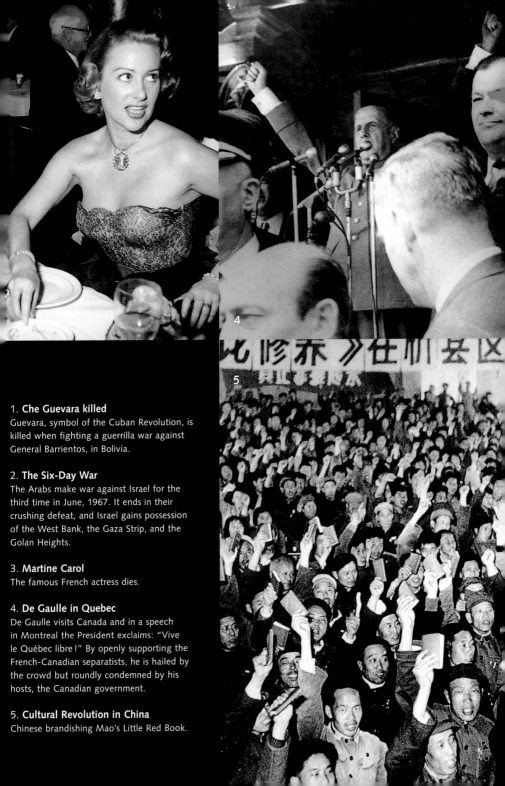

1. Che Guevara killed
Guevara, symbol of the Cuban Revolution, is killed when fighting a guerrilla war against General Barrientos, in Bolivia.

2. The Six-Day War
The Arabs make war against Israel for the third time in June, 1967. It ends in their crushing defeat, and Israel gains possession of the West Bank, the Gaza Strip, and the Golan Heights.

3. Martine Carol
The famous French actress dies.

4. De Gaulle in Quebec
De Gaulle visits Canada and in a speech in Montreal the President exclaims: "Vive le Québec libre!" By openly supporting the French-Canadian separatists, he is hailed by the crowd but roundly condemned by his hosts, the Canadian government.

5. Cultural Revolution in China
Chinese brandishing Mao's Little Red Book.

1970

Second Part

1970

In France, new cars now have to be fitted with seat belts, the wearing of which is compulsory. The French Communist Party elected its new Assistant Secretary-General, Georges Marchais. In Palestine, Yasser Arafat makes it known that he intended to liberate the territory by force. In India, maharajahs' privileges are abolished. After Nasser's sudden demise, Anwar Sadat becomes president of Egypt, and in Chile, the Marxist Salvador Allende is elected president, and intends to introduce radical reforms, including nationalization of property.

In Italy, divorce is finally legalized. After all their box-office hits, the Beatles split up. The incredible music festival at Woodstock in 1969 causes the hippie phenomenon spread like wildfire. New pop stars emerge on a daily basis—Joe Cocker, Bob Dylan, Jim Morrison and the Doors. The feminist movement is gaining ground. In Paris, women organize mass demonstrations.

France and the rest of the world are shattered by the death of the General de Gaulle. The French Vichy politician Édouard Daladier and the Portuguese dictator, Antonio Salazar, follow him to the grave. Literary circles are plunged into mourning by the deaths of John Dos Passos, Jean Giono, François Mauriac, Elsa Triolet, Fernand Crommelynck, and Bertrand Russell. The singers Janis Joplin, Jimmy Hendrix, and Luis Mariano, and the French comedian Bourvil die in turn.

Opposite:
A Spanish bodega.

1970

Vega Sicilia "Unico" 1970

Spanish wine – Ribera del Duero

It is too often forgotten that the Spanish wine region is the largest in Europe. However, if Italy had lost the tradition of great wine-making for a time, Spain had shunned it for even longer, if fortified wines, such as sherry, are excluded. All this changed in 1864, when D. Elay Lecanda y Chaves purchased a strange, fertile plain from the Santos Cecilia family (Cecilia was changed to "Sicilia", Vega means "fertile plain"), part of which was on slopes. The property has also been called Pago de la Vega Santa Cecilia y Carrascul. Lecanda y Chaves was a pioneer, because although phylloxera encouraged many wine-growers from the Bordeaux area to settle in the Rioja and the Duero areas, and thus introduce their vines to the region, this only happened 15 years later, after 1880. Ignacio Herrero was succeeded by Dom Domingo Garramiola as owner of the estate. Gradually, the quality of the huge vineyard improved. However, it was not until as late as 1970 that Vega Sicilia completed its rise and came to be recognized as Spain's greatest wine. It now delights œnogists throughout the world and unselfconsciously asserts its claim to emulate the greatest of the great wines. It opened the way for other Spanish wines, much to the joy of "true" wine-lovers

The story began on the left bank of the Duero. The soils there are of great geological diversity, being sometimes gravelly, sometimes a mixture of clay and limestone, or consisting of red-stained clay. The initial 125 hectares of the property has been supplemented by about 60 more, which are closer to the plain and therefore composed of richer alluvial soils. Most of the vines are of the local variety, Tempranillo, the

Opposite:
a bottle of
Vega Sicilia.

most frequently grown in the DOC Rioja. In fact, the Tempranillo (the name comes from its early ripening, *temprano* meaning "early" in Spanish) grown in Ribera del Duero appears to be the same variety that is called Tinto Fino locally. Some claims have been made, although there is no proof, that Tempranillo and Pinot Noir have a common origin. Whatever the case, Tinto Fino constitutes 60% of the vine stocks on the Vega Sicilia estate. It is complemented by 25% of Cabernet Sauvignon (a substitute for the Grenache usually grown in the Rioja), and there are also a few Merlot and Malbec stocks. All the grapes are harvested by hand.

The wine-making process is traditional; scraping, natural yeasting, and alcohol fermentation at under 30°C (86°F) for ten to fifteen days. The wine is then stored in large vats for the malolactic fermentation. Then the blending begins. The methods used in Vega Sicilia are completely original though, according to some, slightly old-fashioned.

After spending five years in large casks, followed by ten years in barrels, the wine continues to age in bottles for another ten years and sometimes longer. For instance, the 1970 magnums are not to be sold until 2001!

Vines of.
Vega Sicilia.

Organoleptic Description

The wine is created from the following blend: 60% Tinto Fino, 25% Cabernet Sauvignon, 15% Merlot and Malbec. It was neither clarified nor filtered. Despite its age, and because the edges of the disk tend to turn an orange color, this mythical wine is robust. The bouquet is well-developed, melting, spicy, woody, with undertones of tobacco and coffee. The mouth is impressive in its power and strong tannins, though it also has a lively, nervous touch which is surprising in a wine of this age. The end of the mouth is long and complex, indicating that a Vega Sicilia, even though aged fifteen years in wood, does not dry out. A mystery or...a miracle.

Secrets of quality

Old vineyard, small yield, variable climate.

Availability

Two thousand magnums in 2001.

Current price

In 1995, the wine fetched about 62 euros locally.

Apogee
2000-2010.

Comparable or almost comparable vintage: 1964.

Development: best drunk before 2025.

Valladolid
Ribera del Duero

Weather Conditions

In 1970, the winter was cold and the summer very hot. But the heat of the day contrasted with the cool nights, an indispensable combination for achieving the peak of quality. The grapes were thus able to attain complete, but early, ripeness, and were harvested in ideal weather. Outstanding quantity and quality were thus to be expected.

1. A Gathering of Hippies
After the Woodstock Festival, held in the previous year in the United States, the hippie phenomenon began to spread. They came from the United Kingdom, the United States, France, Germany, the Netherlands, and Italy to attend the Isle of Wight pop festival held from 28 through 30 August, 1970.

2. Northern Ireland
Start of the troubles. British army checkpoint in Belfast.

3. Alexander Solzhenitsin
The Russian dissident whose work denounced the Stalinist era, receiving the Nobel Prize for Literature.

4. Rioting in Paris
The events of May, 1968 were repeated on a smaller scale during the 1970s.

5. Yasser Arafat
Yasser Arafat, chairman of the Palestine Liberation Organization, announcing that he will liberate his country by force.

1971

Superstitious people do not miss the opportunity to attribute the Apollo *XIII* disaster to the number 13. It is followed by a perfect landing on the moon by *Apollo XIV*, or rather by LEM *Antares*, and then by the spectacular *Apollo XV* mission, which place the first extra-terrestrial vehicle on the moon. It is electrically powered. Although the Soviets have lost the race for the moon, they are still in the space race. They are the first to build an orbiting space station. However, three Soviet cosmonauts die of asphyxiation during the year because an airlock fails on their space craft, causing it to depressurize. Russian and American rivalry moves to Mars. The American space probe *Mariner IX* orbits Mars as a satellite, while *Mars III* plants a Soviet flag on the Red Planet.

The *Concorde* supersonic passenger plane goes on its first long-distance test flight between Toulouse, France and Dakar, Senegal. The Shah of Iran holds magnificent feast in Persepolis to commemorate twenty centuries of the monarchy. Switzerland finally grants women the vote. In Paris, the old market district of Les Halles is demolished and motorists are force to pay for parking. The Congo (formerly the Belgian Congo) is renamed Zaire ; Bahrain and Qatar proclaim their independence, as part of the creation of the United Arab Emirates. In Spain, Generalissimo Franco announces that King Juan Carlos will succeed him. Louis Armstrong, Igor Stravinsky, Jean Vilar, Coco Chanel, Khrushchev, and Fernandel die.

Opposite:
snow-covered
vines in the Saar.

1971

Scharzhofberg TBA 1971 German wine

Napoleon knew of this wine because, had it not been for him, the Scharzhofberg hill would still belong to the convent of St. Mary of Treves, founded in the sixth century. Napoleon's military and administrative jurisdiction applied French law to this part of Germany which had two consequences for the land and its vineyards. First of all, the property of the clergy was seized and sold in the same way that it had been in Burgundy (and elsewhere) where ecclesiastical vineyards had been made public property and eventually sold to individuals. Secondly, the laws of succession, which would have led to subdivision of the land, were applied to this part of Germany in the same way as they were to Burgundy and with the same results.

The Scharzhofberg hill was thus put up for auction on August 1, 1797 and acquired by Jean-Jacques Koch, the great-great-grandfather of Egon Müller. He purchased only six hectares of the 18 hectares on sale, and created his vineyard on it. When he died, under Napoleonic law, the six hectares were divided between his seven children. Fortunately, one of the sons bought the shares from his brothers and sisters and thus kept the estate whole.

Egon Müller and his family continue to own the seven hectares, but the total area of Scharzhofberg has been increased by nine hectares. This does not mean, however, that the whole vineyard is of uniform quality. Scharzhofberg enjoys a great reputation, due to the combination of the shale soil and the 45° angle of the slope, which offer great possibilities for Riesling grapes. The variety is at the edge of its area of cultivation

Vineyard in the
Saar.

and it is always at this point that the grape varieties produce their best crops. This characteristic of the vine has a disadvantage and an advantage. On the one hand, it is very sensitive to weather conditions meaning that the quality of the wine is not always good. On the other hand, the wines are of incomparable finesse when everything goes well. Egon Müller's vines have certain unusual features. First of all the stock is not grafted onto the root of a different, phylloxera-resistant variety. The vines are old because the vines of the Moselle were almost totally spared the phylloxera epidemic of plant lice for reasons which have never been explained. It is known that phylloxera does not invade sandy soils as it has difficulty in moving through the sand, but this does not apply to a shale soil.

Egon Müller's Rieslings are hard to cultivate because of the steep gradient of the slope, and the density of the plantings (eight thousand plants per hectare) do not leave much room for the grower to move about in. Despite these difficulties, Egon Müller insists on working on his vineyard in the time-honored fashion and shuns chemical treatments. The grape-pickers sort the grapes on the spot. In order to do so, they have two buckets, the first for grapes which have not been botrytised, and the second for bunches destined for the *Spätlese*. The harvest is lightly pressed, the must is filtered by gravity, then slowly fermented in wood for up to two months, when the sugar content is sufficiently high. As soon as the wine appears to have stabilized, it is bottled, without being clarified but after light filtration.

Egon Müller's Scharzhofberg Trockenbeerenauslese (TBA) is only vinified in very small quantities (two or three hundred bottles a year) and only when the vintage permits. This did not happen at all during the 1960s, three times during the 1970s, and only once during the 1980s.

Egon Müller is not responsible for the incredible prices fetched by his wine—he makes the most expensive wine in the world—produced from grapes affected by the "noble rot" because, like the prices for most the "special" German wines, it is fixed at the annual auction in Treves. This the 1971 TBA was sold for DM 510 in 1972. The record price attained by the 1971 TBA Scharzhofberg produced by Egon Müller is perfectly justified however, since this is a fabulous wine.

Vine plants during the dead season.

Organoleptic Description

Anyone who has drunk this wine, if only once, can never forget it. Not only is its pale gold robe unique, but so is its slightly candied citrus bouquet and floral freshness which cannot be found in any other wine. There is also the (balanced) vigor in the mouth which is unequaled. The acidity is so strong that it feel as if it is scouring the teeth, but it is offset by the residual sugar and the bitterness of the citrusy flavor. There is nothing heavy, thick or cloying in this dessert wine, but on the contrary a freshness and natural gaiety, the movement and rapidity of perpetual youth. A modern sweet white wine.

Secrets of quality
Soil type, old vines, severe pruning, tiny yield.

Availability
Extremely rare.

Current price
No transactions.

Apogee
1995.

Comparable or almost comparable vintages:
1959, 1975.

Development:
slow. It will still be excellent in 2015.

Weather Conditions

Most people can still remember the miraculous summer and fall weather in this part of the world. It could not have been bettered. Warm, dry weather until the harvest, with the morning mists of fall to promote the growth of noble rot on the berries which were small, perfectly ripe, and concentrated. The great vintage promised by nature was indeed incomparable to the best of the century for this type of wine.

1

2

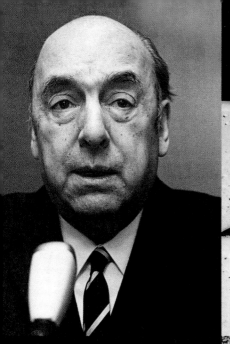

1. Salvador Allende
The recently elected president of Chile accompanied by his daughter.

2. *Concorde*
Concorde leaves France for the first time on a test flight between Toulouse and Dakar.

3. Pablo Neruda
The Chilean poet receives the Nobel Prize for Literature.

4. The Conquest of Space
The first extraterrestrial vehicle is landed on the moon by *Apollo XV*—in the same year, *Mars III* plants the Soviet flag on the Red Planet.

5. War between India and Pakistan
A civil war in the eastern part of Pakistan caused the intervention of India on behalf of the rebels and sends a flood of refugees from East Pakistan into India.

1975

The year was fairly peaceful, with the exception of the escalation of the Vietnam War and civil war in Lebanon. In November, Generalissimo Franco dies, after a 36-year despotic rule, and Juan Carlos de Bourbon becomes king of Spain, undertaking to introduce democracy. In Germany, the Baader-Meinhof gang is brought to justice, marking the end of an era for the anarchist gang. Angola is granted independence by Portugal, and is immediately plunged into civil war, between the government and the rebels supported by South Africa. The OPEC cartel raises the price of oil again, making the oil and gas deposits in the North Sea financially viable, a boon for the economies of the United Kingdom and Norway. In Egypt, after eight years of blockage, the Suez Canal is reopened. The American and Russian space ships, *Apollo* and *Soyuz* meet up and lock together in space.

The Russian physicist and dissident Andrei Sakharov, who had helped to make the Soviet hydrogen bomb, receives the Nobel Peace Prize for his work on human rights. The Soviets consider this to be provocation. A number of artists and performers disappear during the year, including Michel Simon, Pierre Fresnay, Oum Kalsoum, Josephine Baker, Pier Paolo Pasolini, Pierre Dac, Dimitri Shostakovitch, Saint-John Perse, and Gaston Gallimard. Other politicians, apart from Franco, to die that year are Chiang Kai-Shek, Guy Mollet, and King Faisal of Saudi-Arabia who is assassinated.

Facing page:
shaking the bottle.

Clos des Goisses 1975 Philipponnat Champagne

The method used by the estate is similar to that employed by Salon Champagne *(page 132)*, based mainly on five points. Only vintage champagne is produced (so it is not made every year), only grapes of a single provenance are used, the champagne is aged for a long time on its lees—about ten years (although the regulation minimum is three years), production is limited, and the champagne is eventually bottled in a bottle with a distinctive design.

The Clos des Goisses is reflected in the waters of the Marne Canal, and if seen from a distance, the reflection is in shape a champagne bottle lying on its side, a phenomenon that has been responsible for many photographs.

Opposite:
Philipponnat
Champagne cellar.

The road leading from Mareuil-sur-Ay to Tour-sur-Marne separates the enclosed vineyard from the canal. The Clos occupies a very steep slope (about 40%), which was once cultivated using lifting gear, it is so difficult to work. Nowadays, miniature tractors with caterpillar tracks that have been specially designed for this type of vineyard are a useful piece of equipment for working the vines.

The Clos des Goisses, the largest estate in Champagne, was constituted in 1935 by Pierre Philipponnat, who bought plots of vineyard from several different proprietors. It now covers an area of 5.5 hectares. The stock consists of 70% Pinot Noir and 30% Chardonnay. It has exceptional exposure to sunlight, especially as the sun is reflected off the Marne Canal. The must is fermented in neutral vats and in the wood. The wine is then drawn off and stored in special bottles which are sealed

not with a crown stopper (topped with a metal disk), but with one made purely of cork, which explains the expression "tiré sous liège" (drawn off under cork). This means that disgorgement, where the lees that have collected under the cork are drawn off, must be performed by hand, and only after a very long aging period on the fine lees (*dépôt*), a crucial period during which the wine can become more complex after autolysis of the yeasts. The wine-makers describe this phenomenon by saying that "the wine is eating its mother."

The champagne produced by the Clos des Goisses is always made in small quantities. In 1975, the grape harvest was 9,082 kilograms per hectare, a generous yield but not an excessive one. The acidity levels, so important in the balance of a champagne, amounted to 8.5 grams a liter, which was excellent. At the Clos des Goisses, it is usually not necessary to sort the grapes because all the berries ripen every year to a better-than-average, even at the beginning of the harvest. In 1975, however, the grapes had to be sorted which fell even at the beginning of the harvest. The Pinots Noir grapes were exceptional and the Chardonnays added their finesse to the blends.

Above: vines of the Clos des Goisses.

Following pages: Cellar of the Clos *(left);* shaking the champagne bottles to make the sediment collect below the cork *(right).*

Organoleptic Description

Clos des Goisses 1975 seems to be unchanging. Its robe is a uniform gold which hardly changes with age. In fact, it actually looks younger than the 1976 or 1979 vintages. This resistance to the ravages of time is all the stranger when it is remembered that the acidity level is not particularly high. Not only is the 1975 young in appearance, the nose and mouth confirm this impression. The tiny bubbles contribute to the burnt toast and dried fruit bouquet, and in the mouth it has a masterful balance. The whole is melting and harmonious; a pure smooth minerality extends the memory of a full, round champagne without a trace of heaviness.

Secret of quality
Early maturity due to the exposure of the vineyard.

Availability
Over a hundred bottles are still aging in the wine-maker's cellars.

Current price
FF 900 (137 euros).

Apogee
1990.

Comparable or almost comparable vintages:
1952, 1985, 1988.

Development:
should be drunk before 2005.

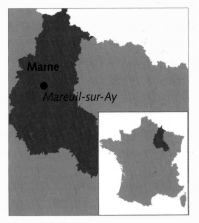

Marne

Mareuil-sur-Ay

Weather Conditions
In 1975, the winter was long and the vegetative cycle began late, full flowering not occurring until around June 25. A very hot, sunny summer made it possible to harvest grapes that were perfectly ripe, however (90% of them exceeded the ten potential degrees, and 30% exceeded 11 degrees). However, in late September, it began to rain, and unfortunately the rain lasted through the harvest, encouraging gray mold and requiring the grapes to be sorted so as to remove any that had rotted.

4

5

1. Conflict in Northern Ireland

Bomb explodes in Dublin.
Ever since direct rule from the United
Kingdom began in 1972, the Irish Republican
Army (IRA) had escalated its operations.

2. The Conquest of Space

Meeting in space between the American
astronaut Stafford and the Soviet cosmonaut
Leonov, when the spaceships *Apollo* and
Soyuz lock together.

3. King Faisal of Saudi-Arabia

Assassination of King Faisal, strong man of
the Arab world and one of the masters of the
international oil supply game.

4. The Baader-Meinhof Gang

The German terrorist Andreas Baader
and his accomplices are caught. The trial
marks the end of this anarchist terrorism.

5. Andrei Sakharov

The dissident Soviet physicist receives the
Nobel Peace Prize for his work in defense of
human rights.

1976

There are two important advances in space exploration. The *Viking I* probe lands on Mars and *Soyuz XXII* becomes the first manned spy satellite. Jimmy Carter is elected president of the United States, probably thanks to the Black vote. Jean Bedel Bokassa becomes Bokassa I by proclaiming himself emperor of the Central African Republic. Two earthquakes in northern China leave 700,000 dead. In France, Jacques Chirac, the prime minister, hands in his resignation to President Valéry Giscard d'Estaing. Raymond Barre takes over. There is a similar event in the United Kingdom with the unexpected resignation of Harold Wilson as prime minister.

In the United States, Patricia (Patty) Hearst, granddaughter of William Randolph Hearst who had been captured by the Symbionese Liberation Army, is seduced by the charms of her jailers and becomes a militant herself. As a result, she is sentenced to 35 years imprisonment, with the right of appeal.

In 1976, The Frenchman Éric Tabarly wins the Transatlantic lone yacht Race on *Pen Duick VI* and at the age of 20, Björn Borg wins Wimbledon.

Mao Zedong dies, having led the Chinese Communist Party since 1921. Other deaths during the year are the novelist Agatha Christie, the physicist Heisenberg as well as Heidegger, Paul Morand, André Malraux, Raymond Queneau, the composer Benjamin Britten, Max Ernst, Fritz Lang, Luchino Visconti, and Jean Gabin.

Opposite:
Rheingau cellar,
Germany.

Hattenheimer Pfaffenberg TBA 1976
Rheingau – German wine

Schönborn castle, in the Rheingau, has been owned by the same family since 1349, but it needed more than tradition for the estate to be preserved, since the parcels of land were not contiguous. Today it covers 75 hectares, the current owner being Karl von Schönborn-Wiesentheid. There are some advantages to being the owner of a winery that dates back to the fourteenth century, such as being able to go down into the cellar and choose a bottle of 1735 in order to auction it at the famous Kloster Eberbach wine auctions. The result is a record price of DM 53,000! The wines of the *Schloss* (castle) Schönborn are numerous and varied, no fewer than fifty varieties, produced by a variety of climates and plots of land. Most of the grapes are Riesling, followed by Pinot Blanc, then Pinot Noir, the latter resulting in a remarkable dark red wine. In addition, harvests that are split or delayed produce special vintages such as the Spätlese, Beerenauslese, Trockenbeerenauslese, and Eiswein. The most valuable wine are harvested from grapes affected by the noble rot, and labeled Beerenauslese and Trockenbeerenauslese (BA and TBA).

Small teams of experts sort the grapes and only pick those affected by the noble rot. Grapes remaining on the vine will eventually be picked, and the grapes that are healthy produce a Spätlese, and even, in some cases, an Eiswein. The harvest is sorted a second time when the grapes are put in a vat, and they are then lightly pressed, the juice being fermented at less than 20°C (68°F). The wine rests on the fine lees for about 20 days, then it's stored in vats for a few more months before being bottled. It's neither clarified nor filtered.

Following pages : wall around the Schloss Schönborn estate.

Organoleptic Description

The 1976 Hattenheimer Pfaffenberg is slightly orange in color, and thick without being oily. The bouquet is very complex consisting of lemony candied citrus and very ripe apricots, with a hint of vanillas. The aromatic complexity is reproduced in the mouth. The wine also has a rare freshness and vigor, which is unexpected in a wine which has attained its apogee. The supreme elegance of a rich wine.

Secrets of quality

Minute yield, draconian selection of botrytised grapes.

Availability

Virtually unavailable (three hundred bottles made).

Current price

Not on the market.

Apogee

1990 to 2000.

Comparable or almost comparable vintages:
1971, then 1979 and 1986.

Development:
drink preferably before 2025.

Schloss Schönborn
● Rheingau

Weather Conditions

In around three years in ten, the weather conditions are good enough to be able to vinify a Trockenbeerenauslese (TBA). *Botrytis cinerea*, the noble rot needed to create this wine, had developed on the grapes which need to be perfectly ripe as the result of a hot summer. Early autumn mists need to dampen the vineyard until the sun breaks through at midday and dries out the grapes.

1

2

4

5

1. Jimmy Carter
After eight years of Republican rule, a Democrat president enters the White House.

2. Éric Tabarly
The French yachtsman wins the Transatlantic Race for the second time, having first won it in 1964.

3. Björn Borg
The young Swede wins Wimbledon at the age of twenty. He would go on to win the French international championship six times and Wimbledon five times.

4. André Malraux
Death of the great French writer. (Photo taken in the early 1940s.)

5. Martin Heidegger
The German philosopher dies this year.

1978

Aldo Moro, former prime minister of Italy and chairman of the Christian Democrat party is kidnaped and assassinated by the Italian Brigate Rosse (Red Brigades). Jimmy Carter reunites Anwar Sadat and Menahem Begin at his presidential country seat, Camp David, for the purpose of signing a peace agreement between Egypt and Israel. In Iran, there are violent demonstrations. The Ayatollah Khomeini is expelled from Iraq and welcomed as a refugee into France. Pope Paul VI dies and is succeeded by John Paul I whose pontificate lasts only 33 days. After his death, John Paul II is elected, the first non-Italian pope for four and a half centuries. In the United Kingdom, the first "test tube baby," Louise Brown, is born, the product of *in vitro* fertilization. The year 1978 is notorious for the worst case of oil pollution in French history, when the oil tanker, *Amoco Cadiz,* runs aground loaded with 230,000 tons of crude oil. A cyclist called Pollentier is disqualified from the Tour de France for drug-taking. The race is won by Bernard Hinault. Other important events are the kidnaping of Baron Empain, Chairman and Managing Director of the firm of Schneider, who is released after having his left earlobe cut off, and the appalling suicide at Jonestown, Guyana of four hundred members of the members of the cult headed by Jim Jones, an American preacher. Jacques Brel and Claude François die; the world of art loses Giorgio De Chirico. Golda Meir, Israel's first woman prime minister, dies in Jerusalem.

Facing page:
a vine starting to
sprout.

Château Rayas 1978
Rhône – Châteauneuf-du-Pape

The French are strong traditionalists in most areas of food and drink, and wine is a classic example of this attitude, especially as vineyards are handed down from father to son. However, a few pioneers have flouted the time-honored rules and shown that truisms can lie.

These "self-taught" wine-makers include Philippe de Rothschild in Bordeaux—patron the Pigalle theater, racing driver, and lover of French literature—Jacques Seysse, a newcomer to the Burgundy district who invented his Morey Saint-Denis and his Clos de la Roche, and Jean Grivot, the pharmacist who has improved the wines of Vosne-Romanée and Gardin, and who left Marseilles to be able to make a better Givry.

Facing page: Château Rayas 1978.

These are just a few of the outstanding figures who bought vineyards with a certain concept of wine-making in their minds, and who were untrameled by the financial and other considerations which can interfere with making wine of the highest quality.

Commander Reynaud, inventor of Rayas, belongs to this category of amateurs and enthusiasts because he is in love with wine, and when love and intelligence are combined, the impossible becomes possible. He is the second generation of Reynauds to own the estate. His father had acquired it by chance, because he was advised to "live in the country" for health reasons. Rayas was not bought for its vines, which had been ravaged by phylloxera. It was his son who created Château Rayas. No tradition, no special knowledge, no esthetic rules had been inherited from his father. In 1920, Commander Reynaud took over the estate and for the next twenty or thirty years completely overhauled the entire

CHATEAU RAYAS

MIS EN BOUTEILLE AU CHÂTEAU

CHATEAUNEUF-DU-PAPE

APPELLATION CHÂTEAUNEUF-DU-PAPE CONTRÔLÉE

CHÂTEAUNEUF DU
VAUCLUSE

FRANCE

vineyard. He must have had a clear plan of what he intended to do and have been very confident of success because he chose the most difficult and constraining methods, which included derisory yields per hectare. It might be thought that he would compensate for the small harvest by extending the area planted with vines because he had quite a few hectares, but he did nothing with them and the woods that surround the small plots of vines contribute to the creation of a micro-climate which attenuates the burning heat of summer at Châteauneuf-du-Pape. He had sought to do this already by choosing north-facing slopes on which to grow the vines. His ultimate aim was to create a fine wine, a wine whose finesse was partly due to the sandy soil in which the vines grew (as opposed to the classic gravel and limestone or clay). Commander Reynaud bet everything on the vineyard—or rather on the grapes—and won. This is surprising because the winestore was very mediocre, especially when compared to his ambitions for the wine.

Landscape around Châteauneuf-du-Pape.

Unlike most varieties of Châteauneuf-du-Pape, the red Château Rayas (there is a rare white of which only two thousand bottles a year are produced) comes from a single variety, Grenache Noir. The Grenache vines are heavily pruned, and harvested "green" in the summer, producing no more than 15 hectoliters per hectare, a derisory amount. The stalks are not removed and are only moderately fermented because at Rayas there is no desire to produce a competition product but a distinguished wine. For the same reason, Château Rayas does not owe its qualities to the wizardry of blending, since the woodiness, vanilla, and tannins contributed by the wood are not sought after.

Is Château Rayas a typical Châteauneuf-du-Pape? Of course not, but the diversity of the soil types and grape variety used might qualify such a hasty reply. At all events, what is quite clear is that this is one of the greatest wines in the world.

Organoleptic Description

The robe does not hide its age, and a slight browning is perceptible in the mass. The finesse and harmony of the aromas are exemplary. The blackcurrant fruitiness is not totally overwhelmed by the tertiary aromas of balsam, reminiscent of Russian leather. In the mouth, the concentration, power, and finesse melt into a supple, almost syrupy, roundness. A wonderfully unique wine.

Secrets of quality
Design of the vineyard, rigorous quality control.

Availability
Rare, the wine has mostly been exported.

Current price
Few transactions.

Apogee 2000.

Comparable or almost comparable vintages:
1967, 1961.

Development: why wait?

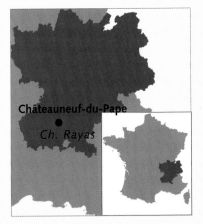

Châteauneuf-du-Pape

Ch. Rayas

Weather Conditions

In the case of the 1978 vintage, the further east-southeast one goes, the better the quality of the wines. They are very acceptable in Bordeaux, excellent in Burgundy, exceptional in the Rhône Valley. Exceptional, because summer and fall were perfect. The grapes were as healthy as they were ripe and they produced one of the best Châteauneuf-du-Pape vintages and an exemplary Château Rayas.

1

2

1. John-Paul II, a Polish pope
For the first time in four and a half centuries, the pope is not an Italian. The Polish archbishop Karol Wojtyla is elected by the 111 cardinals meeting in conclave on October 16, to succeed John Paul I.

2. Black tide
When the *Amoco-Cadiz* oil tanker ran aground, it created another black tide of pollution, this time off Belle-Ile off the Brittany coast. The previous disaster to hit the French coast, the oil spillage from the *Torrey Canyon*, did terrible damage to Finistère, also in Brittany.

3. Bernard Hinault
Winner of the Tour de France cycle race.

4. Anwar Sadat and Menahem Begin
The two leaders signed a peace agreement between Egypt and Israel at Camp David, and jointly received the Nobel Peace Prize for that year.

1982

The Iran-Iraq war continues, and from April through June war is waged in another part of the globe. The Falklands War is started and lost by Argentina which intends to wrest the islands from British ownership. Despite the objections of settlers, Israel returns the Sinai peninsula to Egypt, and then invades South Lebanon, with the aid of the Christian Phalangists. This leads to the massacre of refugees in the Sabra and Shatila camps near Beirut by Phalangist soldiers. Two further terrorist acts arouse universal indignation and horror. In Italy, General Della Chiesa, prefect of Palermo, Sicily is murdered in a car-bomb explosion perpetrated by the Mafia. In France, there is an antisemitic attack in the Jewish quarter of Paris, the Rue des Rosiers, results in six deaths. Still in France, the 39-hour working week is voted in and the French Franc is devalued, while the West German Mark is revalued. France abolishes the law making homosexuality illegal. Gabriel Garcia Márquez receives the Nobel Prize for Literature.

Two leading politicians die Leonid Brezhnev in the Soviet Union and Pierre Mendès France in France. The world of music loses Glenn Gould, Arthur Rubinstein, and Thelonious Monk and the writers Louis Aragon, Pierre Gaxotte and Georges Pérec are no more. Princess Grace of Monaco, Romy Schneider, Henry Fonda, Ingrid Bergman, Jacques Tati, and Rainer Fassbinder also die that year.

Opposite:
a bottle of Pétrus
against a map of
the region.

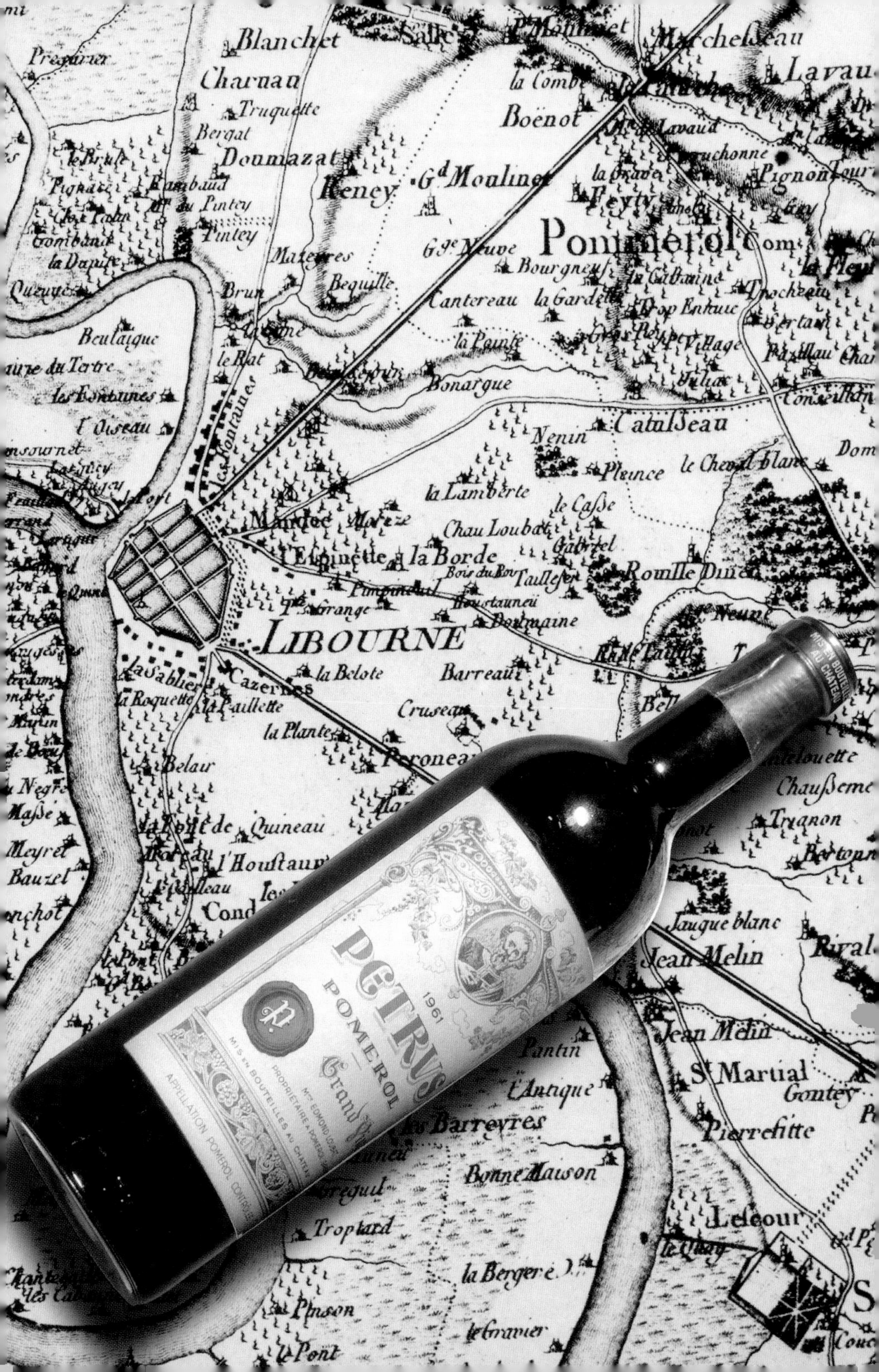

Pétrus 1982 Bordeaux – Pomerol

The reputation of this vintage is well-known. It is also an example of how a vintage can be both great and abundant, although 1982 was no 1961. The grapes were superb, completely ripe, and there was no disparity between alcoholic maturity (sugar) and phenolic maturity (tannins). There was only one blot on the horizon, and it only involved Sauternes (white grapes). The weather was too fine to enable the noble rot to develop on grapes that were nevertheless fully ripe. But as for the red grapes, sugar, ripe tannins and low acidity were all conditions necessary for the creation of a supple and excellent wine. Critics assumed that the resulting wine would be "too good, when, young to have keeping qualities." Pétrus 1982 has given them the lie by its richness in alcohol and abundant tannins.

The Château Pétrus vineyard is one of the most famous in the world. It consists of 11.4 hectares to which five hectares from the neighboring vineyard, the Château Gazin have been added. The soil type is unique, nothing like that on which the other Pomerols are grown. The soil of Pétrus sits like a clay cap or island on an ironstone plinth. The soil would appear to be too compact but it is saved by good drainage and by a stream which only the small area of the vineyard would make it possible to retain. The average age of the vines, of which there are about 6,500 plants per hectare, is about 40 years, among the oldest in the Bordeaux district. They are very severely pruned and the date of harvesting is pondered at length. The grapes are only picked in the afternoon to avoid the dew, and it is performed at great speed, thanks to an army of experienced pickers and carriers. The wine is aged for 22 months in new vats. It is clarified but not filtered.

Organoleptic Description

Despite some of the things that have been said about it, Pétrus 1982 is a powerful, full-bodied, tannic wine whose development is slow, contrary to that of many other vintages of this type. At the heart of an explosive fruitiness there is a strange touch of hardness which is surprising in a wine made exclusively from Merlot. There are successive aromas of the smoothness of plums, mulberries, and a bouquet of spices. The strength and length in the mouth are characteristic.

Secrets of quality
Old vines, soil type, perfectionism.

Availability
The most sought-after vintage after the 1961.

Current price
FF 5,300 (808 euros).

Apogee
From 1995 through 2000.

Comparable or almost comparable vintages:
1947, 1961, 1989.

Development:
preferably to be drunk before 2015.

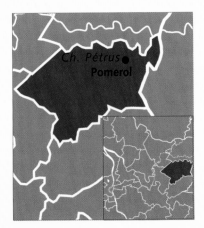

Weather Conditions
The spring was radiant, with early flowering and beautiful, hot summer, with a few small showers which promoted growth. At harvesting time, temperatures were very much in excess of the average (more than 28°C [83°F]).

Pesquera Cuvée Janus Reserva 1982
Ribera del Duero – Spanish wine

It is noticeable that the great achievements in contemporary wine-making—and probably wine-making in the past—are always due to the efforts of a single, strong-minded individual, someone who obstinately imposes his own principles on the prejudices which are too often the result of tradition rather than pragmatism. The creation of a great wine also involves heavy investment, implying that there is a lot of money available. There are numerous examples in the history of the Bordeaux vineyard. Only members of the *parlement*, the assembly of local nobility had the resources to create the Grands Crus, the greatest wines.

The same is true on the other side of the Pyrénées, in Spain's Duero

Facing page:
winestore of the
Alejandro Fernandez
bodega.

Valley, called the Douro where it extends into Portugal.

The man behind this great Spanish wine is called Alejandro Fernandez. After making his money as an industrialist, he realized that his modest family vineyard faced the famous Vega Sicilia estate *(page 242).*
He consequently devised a daring and unreasonable plan to compete with the very best Spanish wine without imitating it.

In 1972, Fernandez created a 65-hectare vineyard, divided into two plots of land that were geologically different. The first was beside the Duero, on gravelly, alluvial soil. The second was on high ground (750 meters above sea level) on a pebbly clay soil, where there was a sharp contrast between day and night temperatures, which is designed to bring out the aroma of the wine.

He only planted the local variety of grape, Tempranillo, at a very low density (2,500 plants per hectare) to make it easy to cultivate the plots.

He also imposed draconian restrictions on the yield per hectare, something that is not easy in a young vineyard.

Vinification left nothing to chance. Although the stalks are normally removed for wines classified as Reserva, in the case of Janus fermentation, the stalks are not discarded but the grapes are picked without their stalks, straight from the vine, in the old-fashioned way. Fermentation is regulated at the exceptionally low temperature of 22°C (72°F) to 25°C (77°F) and maceration is very short (less than ten days). Aging is also unusual, not for the amount of time, which is two years, but for the choice of woods, which consist of 90% American oak, 10% French oak. Although the Vega Sicilia and Pesquera estates are so close to each other, it would be hard to imagine more opposing approaches to vine stocks, vinification, and aging. It is as if Alejandro Fernandez, realizing that he could not compete with Vega Sicilia on his own ground, deliberately chose to take a totally different route with the aim of producing wines that were just as great. The ploy was a complete success. Janus, his prestige wine, which he has been vinifying for less than 20 years, and only when the quality of the vintage so permits, graces the table of the great and the good.

Entrance to the
bodega.

Organoleptic Description

Cuvée Janus 1982 has a wonderful robe. The edge of the disk shows signs of moderate development. The very ripe fruitiness is partially masked by tertiary aromas of tar and leather. The structure in the mouth is imposing, full-bodied, full, but mitigated by an almost syrupy vanilla flavor, contributed by the "American wood." A very interesting composition, combining roundness and virility.

Secrets of quality

Limited yield, careful choice of soil type, and vinification.

Availability

Almost non-existent (about 6,000 bottles, three or four times every ten years).

Current price

Not on the market in Europe.

Apogee 2000.

Comparable or almost comparable vintages: 1985, 1986.

Development: to be drunk after 2010 (perhaps in 2020).

Valladolid

Ribera del Duero

A "competition wine"?

The wine is said to belong to the category of "competition wines" which implies a wine made from overextraction which ages poorly. Yet if the vinifier had sought maximum extraction, he would have opted for long maceration at a high temperature (30 through 33°C [86-92°F]). Under such conditions, and in view of the high tannin content of the Pesquera, the only conclusion is that the Tempranillo varieties, severely pruned, have found their ideal territory.

1

2

1. Iran-Iraq War
Iran launches an offensive against Iraq. The Iraqi president, Saddam Hussein, is shown here visiting the front lines.

2. Gabriel García Márquez
The Colombian writer receiving the Nobel Prize for Literature.

3. Romy Schneider
The Austrian actress died on May 31.

4. Pierre Mendès France
Death of one of France's greatest political figures.

5. Princess Grace
The former Grace Kelly is killed in an auto-mobile accident.

1985

A new, modernizing influence enters the Kremlin, Mikhail Gorbachov, inventor of *perestroika* and *glasnost*. In the United States, Ronald Reagan is elected to his second term of office. The Iran-Iraq war shows no signs of ending. Nor does the Lebanese civil war, of which kidnaping of foreigners has now become a feature. Michel Seurat and Jean-Paul Kauffmann are two Frenchmen who are kidnaped. The Greenpeace ship *Rainbow Warrior* on its way to Mururoa, to protest against French nuclear testing, is sunk in the port of Auckland, New Zealand, sabotaged by French secret agents who are caught and sentenced to ten years in prison. The French minister of defense, Charles Hernu, is forced to resign and is replaced by Paul Quilès. A lot of important projects are in the pipeline in France, including a tunnel under the English Channel and a glass pyramid at the Louvre. Imitating Germany and the Netherlands, French premier Laurent Fabius orders AIDS tests to be introduced for blood donors. In the United Kingdom, the coal miners are finally beaten by Margaret Thatcher and her government after striking for a year against pit closures. There is another soccer massacre, when 38 people are killed and 450 wounded at the European Cup Final at the Heysel Stadium in Belgium. The wreck of the *Titanic* is located. Marc Chagall, Jean Dubuffet, Orson Welles, Simone Signoret, Louise Brooks, Henri Flammarion, James Hadley Chase, Jacques de Lacretelle, René Barjavel, and Michel Audiard die during the year.

Facing page: Moët et Chandon cellar.

Dom Pérignon 1985 Champagne

The nineteenth century was a time when legends were created and enhanced. There was Charlemagne with his long beard, Henri IV of France and his "chicken in every pot," Joan of Arc who personified French nationalism—and Dom Pérignon who "invented" Champagne.

Facing page: bottles of Champagne being aged in the traditional upside down position, so that the lees collect on the cork.

Following pages: harvesting basket for Champagne grapes.

When historians come to examine the facts, however, they find a dirth of information. Dom Pérignon is known to have been born in 1638, the same year as Louis XIV, and to have died in 1715, the year in which the Sun King died. Apart from that, there is little information, a few letters, a few signatures of some standard contracts; nothing has been written about him by his contemporaries, at least until he died. Dom Pérignon was a monk at the Abbey of Hautvillers, near Épernay in the heart of Champagne and from 1668 he was its cellarer-purchasing agent. The abbey owned a large, 25-hectare vineyard and he was perfectly satisfied with its wine and the money it made. Dom Pérignon had a large cellar built which could hold up to 500 bottles of wine, but we do not know what wine it was. According to one of Champagne's best historians, Colonel Bonal, Dom Pérignon never vinified sparkling wines.

According to Fernand Woutaz, who is relying on intuition, the treatise entitled *Manière de cultiver la vigne et de faire le vin en Champagne* (*Manner of cultivating the vine and making wine in Champagne*) published in 1718 by Cannon Godinot, was really written by Dom Pérignon (or rather based on the notes he had made).

One thing is certain, it was the English who first used the "méthode champenoise." A publication dated 1662 describes the method thus:

"Add sugar and molasses to make the wine effervesce." This method was not adopted in Champagne until around 1800. Prior to this date, the fizziness was achieved in Champagne by bottling it too early (a method known as the *méthode rurale*). In 1732, Bertin du Rocheret, the biggest wine-merchant of the period, writes in his notebook: "I do not know if we will [make it] foam."

The first official permission to sell the wine in bottles dates from 1728. This explains why the oldest champagne firm was not founded until 1729 (by Ruinart), which is 14 years after Dom Pérignon's death.

The uncertainties of history, however, do nothing to spoil the merits of Dom Pérignon champagne, which was recognized in his day for white wines of exceptional clarity.

One century later, Eugène Mercier, a prominent figure in the region, who died in 1904, registered the Dom Pérignon trademark and presented it as a gift to Moët et Chandon on the occasion of a marriage. It was not actually used until 1936, when it was launched for the inaugural voyage of the ocean-going liner, the *Normandie*.

The Moët et Chandon estate.

This first Dom Pérignon was the 1921 vintage, one that is so legendary that many œnophiles claim it to be the vintage of the century.

In 1985, the grapes were in perfect health and maturity was ideal. The very mild fall permitted an exceptional second harvest at the end of the month. While it is rare that second generation grapes attain full maturity, this happened in 1985. The natural level of alcohol in the musts attained an average of 10° which is excellent; the level of acidity was 8 to 9.5 gram per liter, an indication of balance and longevity. At the time, the vinifiers recognized that the potential of the 1985 was similar to that of 1975.

Dom Pérignon is the result of a blend of two noble Champagne grapes, Pinot Noir and Chardonnay. The 1985 vintage, like the 1982 and the 1976, used more white grapes, 60% being Chardonnay and 40% Pinot Noir. The wines are always made by malolactic fermentation.

Organoleptic Description

The 1985 Dom Pérignon has a very pale straw-colored robe. The nose consists of a basic burnt toast, with floral overtones, tending toward acacia, with a hint of ivy. In the mouth there is liveliness and vigor, perfect balance, great length and, above all, an admirable finesse, perhaps at the price of a slight lack of roundness. The finesse is accentuated by the extreme youth of this wine which was first marketed in 1992.

Secret of quality

Grapes selected from among the Grands Crus.

Availability

Sometimes sold at auction.

Current price

FF 800 (122 euros).

Apogee 1995.

Comparable or almost comparable vintages:
1982, 1971, 1964 – 1961.

Development:
to be drunk preferably before 2000-2005.

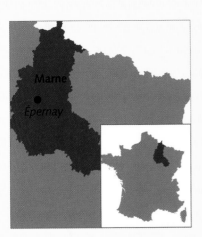

Weather Conditions

In 1985, only half the normal volume of grapes were harvested. The winter temperatures had been the lowest recorded for 150 years (up to - 25°C [13°F]) and frosts in the spring aggravated the situation. But the summer was particularly warm and sunny and in September records were broken. The grapes were harvested between September 30 and October 11.

Sassicaia 1985 Bolgheri – Italian wine

When the renaissance of the great Italian wines, forgotten for more than fifteen centuries, is mentioned, the Sassicaia is generally talked about immediately after Brunello di Montalcino *(page 228)*.

Chance, circumstances, and intuition all combined to give birth to this great wine.

During his student days in the 1920s, the Marquess Mario Incisa della Rochetta planted some French grape varieties in the Asti region. This man of taste appreciated fine French wines and love horseracing. Upon marriage, his wife brought him a huge estates of 2,700 hectares in the Bolgheri region, near Leghorn (Livorno). This is a long way from Tuscany, the home of chianti. During World War II, when it was impossible to get wine from France, the Marquess remembered the Cabernet vines he had planted near Asti. He had them carefully packed and planted one and a half hectares at Bolgheri with them. The vines were severely pruned.

Facing page: winestore of Tenuta San Guido.

The local soil is gravel and the vineyards are at an altitude of 350 meters, guaranteeing some cool weather. Yet the first thousand bottles produced from the new transplanted vines were disappointing. The wine was very tannic and hard, the more so because it had been aged in casks of Slovenian oak. The wine was bottled and stored in the cellar where it was forgotten for a few years. One day, no one knows why, it was tasted again. To everyone's surprise, it was excellent. The wine had digested its tannins, it had "made" and humanized.

As a result, the Marquess decided to plant some more parcels of land

with the grape varieties (more than 25 hectares, planted at a density of 4,000 vines to the hectare) and trained in the French way over short stakes and wires. Giacomo Tachis, the great œnologist who worked for the firm of Antinori, supervised the vinification. The wine-making equipment was perfect; the temperature was regulated at 30°C (86°F) and the fermentation vats were stainless steel. The wine was then aged in French oak barrels.

The wine was given the name of *Sassicaia* which means "poor stony soil" and from 1968, wine-lovers throughout the world were eager to taste the wine.

The Marquess's initiative was very much criticized in Italy, however, partly because the vineyard was located in a region which was not known for its wines, but mainly, because he had not planted the local Sangiovese variety, but foreign vines. The product was a wine that had nothing in common with Tuscan wines, nor even any other Italian wine. The Marquess thus inaugurated a new category of Italian wines which were called, with a degree of contempt, "international wines. "Many other countries have since followed suit. Although Sassicaia had become such a famous wine, it could not be classified as other than a mere *"vino da tavola"* ("table wine") both for the location where it was made and the grape variety used.

When his father died in 1983, the Marquess Nicolo Incisa della Rochetta more than met the challenge. To such an extent that the Sassicaia 1985 has been awarded the prize of best wine in the Cabernet claret category, even when competing against Premier Cru wines from Bordeaux! Fortunately, the Italian authorities are less rigid than their French counterparts and a "Bolgheri" appellation has recently been introduced, a move further justified by the proximity to Sassicaia of another wine that is causing a sensation, Ornellaia, which deserves to be watched as closely as its cousin Sassicaia.

Above: vines of Tenuta.

Following pages: Vega Sicilia, the great Spanish wine *(page 242).*

Organoleptic Description

The 1985 Sassicaia remains the best wine produced from this controversial vineyard. It is a deep ruby color and has just reached its apogee. It is warm, well-built, ample and complex. The tannins are perfectly ripe and expressed in a bouquet of blackcurrant with a hint of licorice, emphasized with tarry and leathery aromas. A woody vanilla binds this harmonious symphony together. In the mouth, there is a supple architecture which does not impose on the melting and complex aromas, with a unique after-taste.

Secret of quality
Combination of climate and soil type.

Availability
Very sought after at auctions in the United States and the United Kingdom.

Current price
No transactions in France.

Apogee
2000.

Comparable or almost comparable vintage: 1985 is indisputably the best vintage.

Development: to be drunk before 2010.

VINO FINO

VEGA-S

BODEGAS Y VIÑEDOS
VEGA SICILIA

TINTO "VALBUENA"

EMBOTELLADO EN SU 5º AÑO

VALBUENA DE DUERO (Valladolid)

BODEGAS Y VIÑEDOS
VEGA-SICILIA

TINTO "VALBUENA"

EMBOTELLADO EN SU 3.ª AÑO

BODEGAS Y VIÑEDOS
VEGA-SICILIA

TINTO "VALBUENA"

EMBOTELLADO EN SU 3.ª AÑO

MARCA
REGISTRADA

VEGA-SICILIA

"UNICO"

COSECHA 1962

Ribera del Duero
Denominación de Origen

Medalla de Oro y Gran Diploma de Honor
Feria de Navidad de Madrid de 1927
Medalla de Oro y Gran Diploma de Honor
Exposición Hotelera de Barcelona de 1927
Gran Premio de Honor
Exposición Internacional de Barcelona 1929-30

13,5 % Vol.

EMBOTELLADO EN LA PROPIEDAD

...A S.A.   VALBUENA DE DUERO (Valladolid) España

ser embotellada

Nº 09546

VINO
DE M...

n uvas: Cabernet Sauvignon

ARCA

VEG

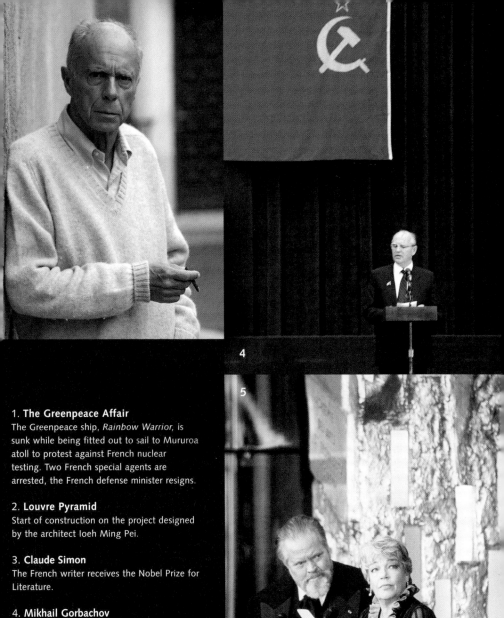

1. The Greenpeace Affair
The Greenpeace ship, *Rainbow Warrior,* is sunk while being fitted out to sail to Mururoa atoll to protest against French nuclear testing. Two French special agents are arrested, the French defense minister resigns.

2. Louvre Pyramid
Start of construction on the project designed by the architect Ioeh Ming Pei.

3. Claude Simon
The French writer receives the Nobel Prize for Literature.

4. Mikhail Gorbachov
The new master of the Kremlin is a modernizer. Gorbachov becomes general secretary of the Communist Party.

5. Simone Signoret and Orson Welles
Both the French actress and the American director and actor, seen here together to award a prize, die this year.

1989

In 1989, the Berlin Wall, erected in 1961, is destroyed forever. The collapse of the Communist world had not been forecast even by the greatest experts. Among those it catches by surprise are the Romanian dictator, Nicolae Ceausescu and his wife, who try to flee. They are caught, summarily tried, and executed. The situation is very different in China, where the television stations of the world all broadcasts the image of a single student blocking the way of a tank during the massacre in Tien An Men Square. In Iran, the Ayatollah Khomeini and the Shi'ite clergy pronounce the death sentence on the British author, Salman Rushdie, for the "blasphemous" content of his book *The Satanic Verses.* A few months later, Khomeini dies at the age of eighty-nine. In his lifetime, he had been responsible for the execution of 50,000 opponents of the regime and a million killed in the Iran-Iraq War. Football is still a killer: at the Hillsborough Stadium in Sheffield, England, police misdirect the crowd as a result of which 94 are crushed to death and nearly 200 wounded. In France, new anti-smoking measures are introduced. In Paris, two major new buildings, the Opéra-Bastille and the Arche de la Défense are inaugurated and the bicentenary of the French Revolution is an excuse for lavish celebrations. There are plenty of celebrity deaths in 1989, including the Emperor of Japan, Hirohito, the painter Salvador Dalí, and the writers Georges Simenon and Samuel Beckett. Bette Davis, the zoologist Konrad Lorenz, and the boxer Ray Sugar Robinson also die this year.

Facing page:
case of Château
Haut-Brion.

Château Haut-Brion 1989
Pessac-Léognan – Bordeaux

A symbolic estate, and one that is unique, because it is the birthplace of claret. In 1525, Jean de Pontac married Jeanne de Bellon. Her dowry included a vineyard at Haut-Brion on the site of the present vineyard, which is now surrounded by the town, and whose grapes are harvested by students from the nearby university campus. The Pontac family took more than two centuries to invent claret as we know it today, a long time before the estates of Margaux, Latour, or Lafite, which also produce great Bordeaux wines and whose owners were once members of the assembly of lords in Bordeaux known as the *parlement*.

The Pontacs introduced two innovations. Firstly, the practice of "tirage au fin," drawing off the wine above the lees, meant that the wine was blended and refined. Secondly, by personalizing the wine which they offered under the name of Haut-Brion, they emphasized its origin and its uniqueness. Shortly after 1600, the Pontacs are said to have invented the concept of a "cru," often mistranslated into English as "growth" which has become an indication of quality. They may have intended it merely to mean a brand name. Clearly the success of claret was not due to a new soil type but to the vinification method. Haut Brion's fame soon spread to England, because in April, 1663, Samuel Pepys— bon vivant and diarist—wrote that he spent the evening at the Royal Oak Tavern: "Where I partook of a variety of French wine called Ho-Bryan which had an especially good and unusual flavor the like of which I had never before encountered." This is the first time a claret is specifically mentioned by its brand name or "cru." Hitherto, wines had been identified only by the region from which they came— Graves, Médoc, etc.

Château
Haut-Brion.

The Pontacs were clearly adopting this as a marketing strategy because, in 1666, they opened a luxury tavern-cum-grocery-store called *The Pontac Head,* at which they sold Haut-Brion. It became the haunt of London high society. Haut-Brion thus had a thirty or forty year head-start on the other Premiers Crus and sold its wine easily and very expensively. Even the French taxation authorities noted that the price of "vin Pontac" was 20-30% higher than that of the next most expensive wine. The fame of the Pontac family in England and the sensation caused by the wine were such that the philosopher, John Locke, decided in 1677 to go and visit the vineyard at Haut-Brion, from which the wine was made. Here he observed:

"A west-facing rounded hill. The soil looks as though it were incapable of producing anything, consisting as it does of white sand mixed with a little gravel." This is an excellent description of Pyrenean Graves soil, a large wine-growing area, which does not alone account for the singularity and supremacy of Haut-Brion at the time. From the early eighteenth century, the best vineyards copied the "Haut-Brion method" and were known by their own names. Subsequently, through marriage, Château Haut-Brion became the property of the Fumel family. The statesman Talleyrand bought it in 1801, then the estate changed hands three times until it was acquired by the American banker, Clarence Dillon, in 1935, at a time when wine-makers were experiencing a crisis due to the Depression. Dillon's granddaughter, the Duchess de Mouchy, now owns this jewel as well as the neighboring château of la Mission Haut-Brion.

The 42 hectares are planted with Cabernet Sauvignon (55%), Merlot (25%) and Cabernet Franc (20%) at a density of 6,000 plants per hectare. Jean-Bernard Delmas, manager of the estate, equipped Haut-Brion with computerized vinification equipment and stainless steel vats and pipes, at the cutting edge of progress. The wine is fermented in vats for 40 days, and is then aged in new wood (like all the Premier Cru wines). It is then clarified, lightly filtered, and bottled in old-fashioned flagon-type bottles. The year 1989 was a great one for all the wines of Bordeaux, even the dessert wines. This was the result of perfect harvests which lasted from late September through late October. The red grapes needed more care than the whites, however, because the makers had to deal with three problems. Alcoholic maturity (due

to proportion of sugar) occurred earlier than the phenolic maturity (tannins), so that those wine-makers who harvested too early missed the opportunity of creating a great wine. Furthermore, late flowering without any damping off and optimum conditions meant the harvest would be abundant, almost untouched by the summer drought. Consequently, if harvesting was not performed early, the great potential of the 1989 vintage was diluted. On the other hand, if the grapes were harvested too late, they suffered from one of the failings of which the 1989 wine is often accused, namely too low an acidity level. One wine-maker realised

The winestores of the estate.

he had too many grapes and tried to concentrate the wine but all he obtained was a diluted wine with low acidity. Jean-Bernard Delmas committed no such error. His early harvest was exemplary and he left the tannins to mature perfectly. The result was soon obvious. Long before it was bottled, the 1989 Haut-Brion was considered to be the best wine to have been vinified on the estate since 1961.

Organoleptic Description

How can such a perfect wine be described? 100% concentrated, 100% balanced, 100% harmonious, 100% complex, with the addition of the characteristics which are unique to Haut-Brion, the hint of smokiness and the balsamic touch contributed by masterful blending.

Secrets of quality

Perfect grapes, yield problems overcome.

Availability

Star of the wine auctions and resellers.

Current price

About FF 1,000 (152 euros).

Apogee
2000.

Comparable or almost comparable vintages:
1961, 1990.

Development:
to be drunk in the next 20 to 25 years.

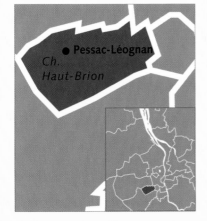

Weather Conditions

In 1989, the hot weather started early. The wine-lovers who attended the Vinexpo trade show in Paris in June that year remember the unbearable heat (38°C [100°F]) which led to the installation of air-conditioning in the Palais des Expositions. The white grapes were harvested before the end of August and the first red grapes were picked in early September. A few showers fell around September 10.

Barbaresco Sori San Lorenzo 1989
Italian wine

Italian viticulture has several distinctive features. The tradition is a long
one and wines have been produced whose reputation has lasted over
the centuries. Italy is the birthplace of European (and thus world)
viticulture, but, curiously, for nearly 2,000 years, there has been no
desire to create great wines. It was not until the late nineteenth century
that a grower first revived the production of quality wines.

In practice, however, it was not until after World War II that Italian
wine-makers revived their dormant lands. The resurrection is due to a
few prominent personalities with boundless energy, of which Angelo
Gaja is the archetype.

*Facing page:
bottles of Gaja.*

The Gaja family left Spain and settled in Piedmont in the seventeenth
century. In 1859, they began making and trading in wine, buying
vineyards in the Barbaresco region and, according to custom, also
buying in grapes. In 1961, Angelo Gaja decided to move the family
enterprise forward in a new direction. A few years later, he took the
crucial decision to sell his wine only in bottles. In 1973, he tried
unsuccessfully to sell his wine to the United States. Yet since 1970 he
had had an important asset, a very skilled œnologist (chief cellarer),
Guido Rivella, a wine-maker whose talent was proved by the sequel.
What is wrong with a Barolo and a Barbaresco? They are too hard, they
contain too much tannin and too much acidity and the end of the
mouth is dry.

Angelo Gaja, who was well-traveled and had tasted wines from all over
the world, drew conclusions which might seem paradoxical, namely that

GAJA

BAROLO
ZIONE DI ORIGINE CONTROLLATA E GARA

SPERSS
1990

13,5% BY VOL., BOTTLED BY GAJA, BARE
RED WINE, PRODUCT OF ITALY

GAJA

BARBARESCO
OMINAZIONE DI ORIGINE CONTROLLATA E GARANTITA
SORÌ TILDÌN
1990

the yield per hectare should be halved and the harvest should be late when the grapes were fully ripe. The fermentation and aging periods should be shorter, and the vats should be replaced by casks.

This seems to be illogical because reducing the yield would concentrate tannins. In fact, the reality is very different. Reducing the yield per hectare balances the must, increasing the aromas without increasing the tannins, and improving the quality. Furthermore, the casks were heavily scalded to reduce their tannic contribution (the water that poured out was very brown). Aging in casks, however, produced measured oxidation, something that is needed to make the wine "rounded."

It is no surprise to learn that in Piedmont, Angelo Gaja was taken for a madman, a criminal revolutionary who would ruin the region by imposing green harvests. Gaja took no notice and persevered. Today, in addition to his Barbaresco vineyard, he has acquired a property in Barolo, and another at Montalcino, with a view to producing Brunello, as well as 70 hectares (to be planted) in the new Bolgheri appellation—right beside the famous vineyards of Sassicaia and Ornellaia.

Vines on the estate.

The creation of great wines is only achievable by discovering how best to use the best land for vineyards. In the Barbaresco DOCG, Angelo Gaja isolated three plots which he vinified separately. In 1967, it was the Sori San Lorenzo, in 1970, the Sori Tildin and, in 1973, the Costa Russi. All these wines were made from Nebbiolo, a very old and very great grape variety, native to Piedmont, which was used for making Barolo wines in the sixteenth century and even as early as the fourteenth century. Some claim it was even used by the Romans.

Organoleptic Description

Barbaresco Sori San Lorenzo 1989 of Gaja is a work of art. The robe is impressive almost unmarked by the passage of time; the complex bouquet of very ripe almost cooked, red berries, marries with a touch of violet, smoke, and leather and tends to the dark and somber. The woodiness is not invasive and contributes a light, balsamic binding note to the aromatic components. The structure in the mouth is strong, the tannins being both thick andvigorous, ensuring that this slow developing wine will have wonderful keeping qualities.

Secrets of quality

Limited yield, maturity and vinification suited to the wine.

Availability

Variable, depends on the country. Not easy to find outside Italy.

Current price

FF 800 (122 euros).

Apogee
2010.

Comparable or almost comparable vintages:
1961 (old style), 1988, and 1990.

Development:
should be drunk before 2030.

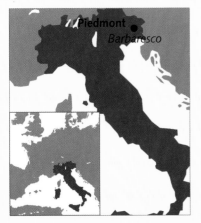

Weather Conditions

This type of wines deserves more in-depth study because it accumulates the greatest amount of tannins and maximum acidity, hence the importance of the exposure of the vines. Furthermore, it should be noted that Nebbiolo is a late-maturing variety, so it is vital that the fall weather should be clement, even hot and sunny. This was the case with the 1988, 1989, 1990 vintages.

Montrachet 1989 Burgundy

"Montrachet! Divine Montrachet! The first and finest among white wines
(…)." Thus wrote the Marquis de Cussy in the nineteenth century.
Montrachet, like Corton-Charlemagne, is one of the greatest dry white
Burgundies. The two wines are historically—or legendarily—very different.
Corton-Charlemagne took the name of the Holy Roman Emperor in 775,
when the "clos Charlemagne" vineyard was donated to the collegiate
church of Saulieu at Aloxe. According to legend, the vineyard also owes its
white grape varieties to Charlemagne, because his wife, Barbe, hated

Facing page:
entrance to the
Château de Beaune
estate.

seeing her husband stain his magnificent beard with red wine! The history
of Montrachet is not nearly so glorious or ancient. It was not until 1728
that the Abbé Arnoux, one of the greatest œnophiles of the period, noted
its existence, claiming with complete justification that it was the "most
unusual and delicate wine in France." Clermont-Montoison, who was a
member of a family of noble lineage related to the Clermont-Tonnerres,
realised the importance of the estate when he married the heiress to the
barony of Boutière in 1710, and thus becoming lord of Chassagne and
owner of the castle of Chagny. He added to his holdings by acquiring more
land until he owned half of Montrachet. In 1776, a Clermont-Montoison
married Charles de la Guiche and half of Montrachet thus passed to that
family. During the French Revolution, Charles de la Guiche was guillotined
and his lands sold as national property, but the family eventually managed
to buy it back. The family changed its name to become de Laguiche after
the Revolution, and still owns the entire estate, with the exception of two
hectares that were sold to Bouchard in 1838. This jealously preserved plot of

land offers production conditions that are as perfect as they are rare, if not unique. But anyone looking for a picturesque hill at Montrachet will be disappointed. The word "rache" means "scurvy" or "bare,"and it is indeed a bare hillock topped with one or two ragged trees. The vines grow lower down the hill. First there is the vineyard of Chevalier-Montrachet then just below it the royal vineyard of Montrachet. It is not too high and not too low, in a balanced position. Bâtard-Montrachet is right next to it, covering the opposite side of the hill. As for the soil, the whole mystery of the wine is here. It is hard to explain because so many factors are at play that it would be impossible to list them all, especially as the way in which they interact increases the difficulty of doing so. The layer of topsoil is very thin. Just below it there are gravel and limestone alluvial deposits and it is these which are of prime importance. There is much more active limestone (13 %) here than anywhere else in Burgundy. The stony soil ensures good drainage, reduces erosion, and stores the heat.

The Montrachet vineyard is split up and always was. The Laguiche family owned half of it and they currently own a quarter, making them the largest landowners. In 1838, Bernard and Adolphe Bouchard bought part of the Laguiche holding. Today, the firm of Bouchard owns only 0.89 hectare because, in 1845, Adolphe, in a fit of generosity, donated his share of Montrachet to a female friend; this part now belongs to the Ramonet and Laguiche families and the Boillerault heirs. The parcel of Montrachet which belongs to the firm of Bouchard is in the commune of Puligny-Montrachet, in the heart of Montrachet, between the Chevalier and the Bâtard. Harvesting is performed by hand, vinification in the traditional way, fermentation and aging, then racking in bottles.

Above: cellar in the château.

Following pages: Montrachet *(left);* Corton Charlemagne *(right).*

Organoleptic Description

Visually, Montrachet 1989 is uniform in color. Aromatically, there are fragrances of honey and almond with a woody aroma that is eventually predominant. The woodiness is also elegantly present in the mouth with power and suppleness. The construction is rigorous, a measured nervosity which ensures balance and does not prevent the development of this wine is about to reach its apogee. It has a measured sagacity.

Secret of quality

Maturity of the grapes.

Apogee
2004.

Availability

From cellars and wine auctions.

Comparable or
almost comparable
vintages:
1983, 1985, 1992.

Current price

FF 1,000 (152 euros).

Development:
to be drunk before
2025.

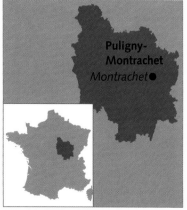

Puligny-
Montrachet
Montrachet●

Weather Conditions

Heat may also be one of the secrets of Montrachet. There is a perfect south-southeastern exposure, so that not a calorie is lost, from the first to the last rays of the sun. The vine is grown on a gentle slope (10‰), whose wild flora are of a type found elsewhere only much further south. March 1989 was a particularly mild month so the vegetative cycle began early. A cold spell in April slowed it down again but the fine weather returned and flowering was early though prolonged. July was hot and stormy, but August was dry and the heat resulted in early harvesting (around September 15), under excellent conditions, producing a crop of healthy, ripe grapes.

1

2

4

5

1. Grande Arche de la Défense
Inauguration of the massive arch designed by Johan-Otto von Spreckelsen to house the French Ministry of Defense in Paris,

2. Bicentennial of the French Revolution
A huge and lavish parade is organized along the Champs-Élysées in Paris to mark the great occasion.

3. Samuel Beckett
Death of the Irish poet and playwright who wrote in both French and English.

4. Fall of the Berlin Wall
Demolition of the wall erected in 1961 symbolizing the collapse of the Communist block. The frontiers of the GDR opened and Berliners streamed out to the West.

5. The Beijing Spring
In May, thousands of students demonstrated on Tien An Men Square, demanding freedom and democracy. On June 4, the military stepped in. The official death toll was 1,400, though there were nearly 3,000 casualties.

1990

Three major political events make this a year to remember: the reunification of Germany, the Iraqi invasion of Kuwait, and the resignation of Mrs. Thatcher. The first elections for the whole of Germany are held at the end of the year, which are won by Helmut Kohl and his Christian Democrat party.

Proof emerges that the alleged massacre at Timisoara, in Romania, was a ploy invented for television news purposes.

Lech Walesa, charismatic leader of Solidarity, is elected Polish head of state, by an unsurprising 75% of votes.

Since the death of Tito, Jugoslavia has become increasingly unstable. Serbia orders the dissolution of parliament and of the regional government of Kosovo, whose Albanian ethnic population has rebelled against Belgrade's authority.

Iraq's invasion of Kuwait in early August will unleash the Gulf War at the beginning of the following year. The United Kingdom and Argentina restore diplomatic relations, broken off during the Falklands War. The last of the subcompact 2 CV cars roll off the Citroën production line in France. Mikhail Gorbachov wins the Nobel Peace Prize. Two French politicians, Charles Hernu and Jacques Soustelle, die. Literature loses Alberto Moravia. In the United States, the psychologist Bruno Bettelheim dies, as do Ava Gardner, "The Barefoot Contessa," and the divine and mysterious Greta Garbo, who had not made a film since 1941.

Facing page:
bottles of Veuve
Clicquot
champagne.

Veuve Clicquot Grande Dame 1990
Champagne

The Widow Clicquot must be the most famous Frenchwoman in the
world, after Joan of Arc. Her Champagne has won her great renown,
amplified and sustained by her powerful personality, which was much
ahead of her time. Her husband provided her with her first innovation,
a distinction in Champagne—he made her a widow. This gave her total
autonomy over the estate, something that was extremely rare in 1805.
At the age of 21, she married François Clicquot-Muiron, who worked

Opposite:
bottles of
champagne
maturing.

with her father, a banker and draper who also dabbled in selling some of
the wine produced at his vineyard in Bouzy. She had only been a widow
for a few months when, at the age of 27, she founded the Veuve

Following pages:
the Veuve Clicquot
cellar.

Clicquot-Ponsardin company, combining her maiden name with that of
her late husband. She rehired Bohne, the cellarer, who had worked in
the previous company and sold about 50,000 bottles a year. Veuve
Cliquot ran her enterprise with great authority. She is alleged to have
invented a type of table on which to shake the champagne, forerunner
of the triangular "schooldesks" (*pupitres*) which are now used. This is
not quite true because the tables had been invented about 40 years
earlier, but she is probably the first to have used them for "mass"
production. It is even claimed that she "invented" pink champagne,
which she made a speciality of the house, a tradition that continues.
However, it appears that in 1777 (a year before the future Madame
Clicquot was born), Philippe Clicquot-Muiron, her future father-in-law,
was selling pink champagne to his customers. After her husband's death,
Nicole Clicquot continued to buy vineyards with astonishing discernment

and her holdings finally constituted a huge vineyard as interesting in the diversity of its vines as in their quality.

Her daughter married Count de Chevigné, a charming man of letters, sophisticated and delightful but a poor businessman, who tried to involve his mother-in-law in various other activities, such as banking and drapery, at the risk of compromising the prosperity of the company. Fortunately, Madame Clicquot employed Edouard Werlé as a business manager who, unlike her son-in-law, proved to be an excellent manager. The enterprise prospered hugely and was soon producing more than 500,000 bottles a year. The widow Clicquot was very fond of her son-in-law and it was no doubt it was he who persuaded her to acquire the old Château de Boursault and restore it into a magnificent castle overlooking the river Marne. It is here that Madame Nicole Cliquot died at the age of eighty-eight, after making all the arrangements necessary to protect the interests of her daughter and enable her firm to go to the heirs of the Werlé family with which she was associated. For a century,

the Werlés ran the Veuve Clicquot-Ponsardin company with great success, until it was acquired by the LVMH group.

The year 1990, was an early one, and the harvest was abundant. The musts were surprisingly rich (10.7 degrees) and nicely acidic (8 g per liter), a sign of excellent Champagnes to come. This was confirmed by the Cuvée Grande Dame 1990, the result of a blend of the eight best Grands Crus. Verzenay, Verzy, Ambonnay, Bouzy, and Ay contributed the black grapes (61%), Avize, Oger, and Mesnil-sur-Oger contributed the white grapes (39%). Obviously, it would have been hard to do better. The Cuvée Grande Dame is a luxury champagne.

Grapes used to produce Veuve Clicquot Champagne.

Organoleptic Description

The wine-maker's maxim, "Give me good grapes and I will make you good wine" is amply proved by the quality of La Grande Dame 1990. The acidity stimulates the aromatic richness, and the carbon dioxide is perfectly integrated. The champagne has a generosity, roundness, suppleness, and length in the mouth which contribute to the versatility of this champagne. It can be drunk alone, or with food and it is full-bodied enough to blend well with numerous dishes.

Secret of quality
Record amounts of sunshine.

Availability
Still being sold.

Current price
FF 500 (76 euros).

Apogee
2000.

Comparable or almost comparable vintages:
1955, 1959, 1985.

Development: preferably to be drunk before 2005.

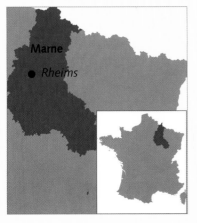

Weather Conditions

The year 1990 can be considered an early one. Budding began in late March, and flowering in early June. The harvest began on September 11. Although there had been a frost in early April, the harvest was abundant (12,000 kg). The weather in July, August, and the first three weeks of September was ideal, to such an extent that the sunshine records for the previous thirty years were beaten!

1

2

1. Lech Walesa
The leader of the Solidarity Trade Union and winner of the Nobel Peace Prize in 1983 is elected President of Poland with 75% of the votes.

2. Channel Tunnel
On December 1, the French and British sections join up, marking the "end" of Great Britain's isolation as an island.

3. Greta Garbo
Death of the famous Swedish-born actress, nicknamed "the Divine."

4. Opéra Bastille
The new Paris opera house was opened to mark the two hundredth anniversary of the Carlos Ott.

5. The Gulf War
The Iraqi army invaded Kuwait and held all the key positions on August 3. On November 30, the United Nations Security Council decides to intervene militarily to stop the Iraqi dictator and drive him out.

1994

A severe earthquake hits the western suburbs of Los Angeles. Richard Nixon dies. A new president, Bill Clinton, brokers peace in the Near East by getting Israeli prime minister Yitzhak Rabin and PLO chairman Yasser Arafat to shake hands and sign a peace agreement. Rabin and Arafat share the Nobel Peace Prize with former Israeli prime minster Shimon Peres. In South Africa, Nelson Mandela is elected president, but genocide erupts again in Rwanda. In Italy, Silvio Berlusconi, the media mogul, becomes prime minister after his party, Forza Italia, wins an absolute majority in the lower house after the elections in late March. By the end of December, he is handing in his resignation to the Italian president when it looks as if his party will lose their parliamentary majority. Robert Hue is elected secretary-general of the French Communist Party. The Channel Tunnel is opened and it is the fiftieth anniversary of the Normandy Landings which liberated France from German occupation. The playwright Eugène Ionesco, the actor, Jean-Louis Barrault, and the singers Jean Sablon and Cab Calloway die, as do the painter Paul Delvaux, the medical researcher Linus Pauling, Jackie Kennedy-Onassis, and Pierre Boulle (author of *The Bridge over the River Kwai* and *Planet of the Apes*). American viticulture loses Tselitcheff, one of its founding fathers.

Facing page: a case of Diamond Creek.

Diamond Creek Lake 1994 Californian wine

Mention American wines to a Frenchman and you are likely to provoke all kinds of contradictory, unpredictable, and often irrational reactions. Certain points should therefore be remembered in order to avoid false assumptions. America is like Italy, in that wine is made in 90 percent of the states. Even though the œnology department of the University of California at Davis is not the greatest in the world, it is still one of the best. Strangely, the United States is not among the so-called "new" producers of wines; American wines were winning medals in Paris exhibitions as long ago as 1900.

Prohibition, that great victory of American womenhood, which was sick and tired of seeing their housekeeping money disappear into the saloons and of being beaten senseless by drunkards, gave rise to smuggling and speakeasies, and although it lasted for "only" 14 years (1919 through 1933) it was followed by the Depression that began in 1929, after which came World War II. For the United States, the cæsura can thus be said to extend for a thirty-year period (1919-1945/1950).

The true enemy of American viticulture, however, was phylloxera, a plague which no one knew anything about at the time. Without these plant-lice, the *Vitis vinifera* vines would have prospered as soon as Thomas Jefferson was returned to office in the nineteenth century. The United States could have explored the land that was suitable for grape-growing and started producing quality wines. So it was not until after World War II that the vineyards of the United States came into their own.

There is no point in dwelling at length on the pre-eminence accorded to
the grape variety, the subject is of marginal importance because a wine
is the product of a combination of the vine stock and the territory. This
is proved by the way in which Al Brounstein has worked his Nappa
Valley vineyard, where the land has been divided into small, individual
parcels, with the aim of producing different wines in each, a policy that
is pursued diligently. Al Brounstein is a gentleman-farmer and an
esthete. He has embraced viticulture like some people embrace religion,
acquiring 16 hectares at the foot of Diamond Mountain. He observed
the geological diversity of the terrain and decided to take advantage of
it in order to produce a variety of wines—a very Burgundian reflex.
Four different wines are made. Volcanic Hill, on 3.2 hectares of volcanic
rock soil (full southern exposure); Red Rock Terrace, on 2.8 hectares of
iron-rich, red earth (north-facing); Gravely Meadow, a vineyard located
between the previous two; and last but not least, Lake, so-called because
the vines grow near a small lake. This parcel (3,000 sq. m.) is only
one-sixth the size of the Romanée-Conti vineyard. As the supreme
affectation, the grapes are only vinified separately if the year is

exceptional (as happened in 1978, 1984, 1987 and 1994). The yield thus represents about 1,500 bottles, which are only produced once or twice a decade and it is the reason why Diamond Creek Lake is the rarest and most expensive wine in the United States.

Despite his Burgundian disposition, Al Brounstein has not tried to make burgundy. He did not plant Pinot, which is only at home further north, in Oregon. He has opted for Bordeaux vines, 88% Cabernet Sauvignon, 8% Merlot, 4% Cabernet Franc. The Lake parcel consists purely of Cabernet Sauvignon.

Unlike in the other vineyards, irrigation stops as soon as the new growing season begins, on April 25. Harvesting is by hand, permitting an initial grading process, and supervision continues because the stalks are also removed by hand. Vinification is Burgundy style in wooden vats (though, unlike in Burgundy, the wood used is Sequoia [Redwood]). Testing and measuring are performed every ten days. The liquid that runs off from the vats and the pressed wine are then mixed in wooden

French hogsheads (new in the case of Lake, 50% new wood in the case of the other wines) and the wine is aged for almost two years, being drawn off four times. The final bottling is performed with complete respect for the wine, which is neither clarified nor filtered.

Vines growing near
Calistoga,
California.

Organoleptic Description

"Lake" is all harmony and finesse. It has "grain" and its tannins are perfectly ripe, not harsh or astringent. It is complex, long, silky, supple, and totally civilized.

Secrets of quality

37.5 hl per hectare, selection, soil type.

Availability

Anyone who has bottles keeps them (production: 1,500 bottles).

Current price

Not on the market.

Apogee
Possibly 2006.

Comparable or almost comparable vintages:
1984, 1987.

Development: slow.

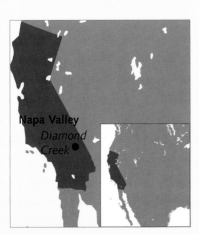

Napa Valley
Diamond Creek ●

Does it match up to the greatest of the great?

When Diamond Creek Lake 1994 was tasted and compared with a 1983 Château Lafite, Lake was found to be as good as a wine which has often been dubbed the First of the First.

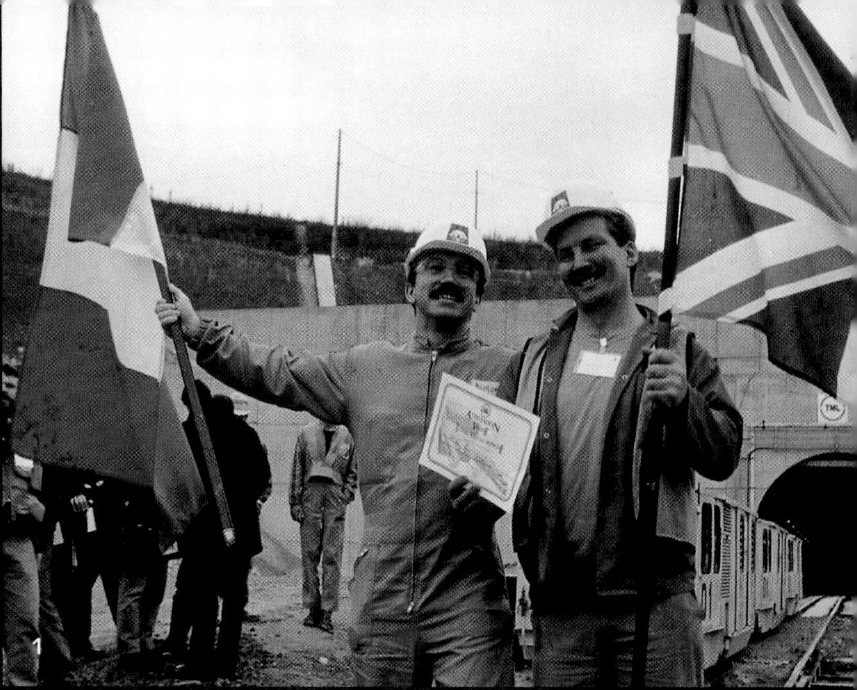

1

2

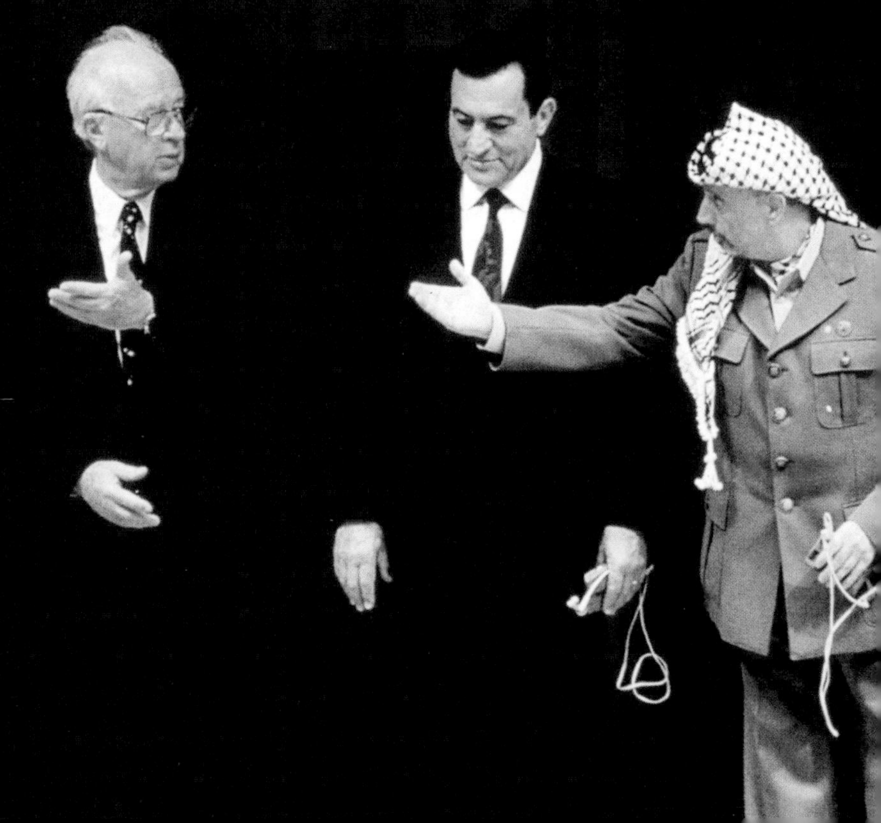

1. The Channel Tunnel
The Channel Tunnel was inaugurated on May 6 by French President François Mitterrand and Queen Elisabeth II. The *Eurostar* now makes it possible to travel by train from London to Paris in two and a half hours, door to door. The trip through the Tunnel takes 20 minutes.

2. Peace in the Near East
Signatories to the Near East Peace Treaty, including Yitzhak Rabin (Israel), Hosni Mubarak (Egypt) and Yasser Arafat (Palestine).

3. Nelson Mandela
Nelson Mandela wins nearly 63% of the vote in South Africa's first multiracial elections.

4. Conflict in Bosnia
Intervention of the UN blue berets.

5. Ayrton Senna
Ayrton Senna, wins the Formula One Grand Prix in São Paulo. The Brazilian racing driver was killed in the same year on the Imola circuit, in Italy.

4

5

1995

Jacques Chirac had been defeated for the presidency of France in 1981 and 1988, but finally succeeds François Mitterrand in the Élysée Palace. In Paris, a bomb explodes in the Saint-Michel subway station, the death toll is 700 and there are 110 injured. The government devises an anti-terrorist plan. In Japan, there is terrifying attack on the Tokyo subway by a religious cult using asphyxiating gas. There are 20 dead and 5,500 gas victims. The Ukraine agrees to close down the Chernobyl nuclear power plant in return for aid from the West of $600 million. In Zurich, drug addicts are "expelled" from a park where they were tolerated hitherto. The Ebola virus ravages Zaire. Ireland holds a referendum as a result of which divorce is legalized. In Poland, Lech Walesa loses the presidential elections and is replaced by Kwasniewski, an ex-communist. Princess Diana gives a television interview in which she admits to having had extramarital affairs. The Queen expresses a wish that the royal couple divorce. Speculation by one of its agents in Singapore causes the venerable two-hundred-year old Baring Brothers Bank to go into liquidation. Emir Kusturica wins the Palme d'Or at the forty-eighth Cannes Film Festival for his film *Underground*. In 1995, the father of *musique concrète*, Pierre Schaeffer dies and so does the actress, Lana Turner, the pianist Arturo Benedetti Michelangeli, the movie director Louis Malle, the explorer Paul-Émile Victor, and the veteran racing driver Juan Manuel Fangio of Argentina. Israel premier Yitshak Rabin is assassinated.

Facing page:
old bottles of Tokay
in a cellar.

Tokay Aszü Oremus 1995 Hungarian wine

The mere name of this wine, which was the court wine par excellence, is worthy of respect. The Tsars of Russia and the House of Hapsburg owned vineyards on the slopes beside the river Bodrog. The river made a vital contribution because, without it, *Botrytis cinerea*, the mold whose presence is indispensable for the vinification of a sweet dessert wine, cannot develop.

Tokay Aszü is one of the oldest dessert wines in the world (do not confuse dessert wines with sweet wines). It is made in a very special way which was described as long ago as 1631. The complex vinification has something in common with the methods employed in Rust to vinify the Ausbruch *(page 146)*, though the latter may have been devised earlier, and the process is reversed. The practice of vinifying botrytised grapes caused a religious dispute, since the Roman Catholic world refused to use "impure"—rotten— grapes which were perfectly acceptable to the Lutherans. The process begins during the harvest. The harvesting system of sorting the grapes by picking only those that are rotten and going along the rows several times, as in Sauternes, is not practiced. Harvesting is late and the grapes are sorted at the end of each row of vines by using the "two-bucket" method used in Germany. The first bucket is reserved for completely rotten grapes, the second for the others. In the fermentation plant, the rotten grapes are loaded into an upright half-hogshead which has a hole at the bottom from which a very sweet juice flows. This juice is not the result of pressing, but of the weight of the grapes pressing on each other. This is called the *eszencia*.

Casks of Tokay
Aszü.

This very sweet liquid hardly ferments at all, the degree of alcohol never exceeding 2 or 3°. It is thus not a wine, but rather a sugary, acid drink which can only be drunk in very small quantities (1 to 3 centiliters). Bottles of this nectar, this quintessence, are rare and very expensive. Tokay Aszü and Tokay Eszencia are the origin of the reputation of the wines of Tokay, which are vinified when the eszencia has run off. The grapes in the half-hogshead are pressed and worked until a paste is obtained whose volume is measured in puttonyos. A puttonyo is a 25-liter container. The content of between three and six of these puttonyos—the number used is stated on the Tokay Aszü label. If more than six are used (between seven and nine), the result is a Tokay Aszü Eszencia, the finest quality wine.

Once vinified, the wine is aged in small wooden casks, in cellars which are really tunnels dug in various parts of the countryside. The style of aging is quite unique and has been the subject of numerous discussions. For traditional aging, maximum oxidation is required. In order to achieve this effect, a little wine is removed from each cask so as to increase contact with the air. After three or four months, the casks are topped up again and aging continues for as long as ten to fifteen years! In the past, the half-liter bottles were stacked up and became covered in mold because the damp atmosphere of these underground tunnels favors their development. Nowadays, however, contemporary taste does not favor oxidation, so the oxidative phase of aging has been abolished, as has very long aging.

This historic wine and its vineyard had its share of problems during the second half of the twentieth century. Communist rule for more than forty years left the cellars and vineyards in poor condition. The estates were nationalized, the vineyards produced on a single type of wine, and the cellars were completely emptied. Yet two great vintages emerged from this period, 1956 (ironically, since it was the year of the Hungarian Uprising), and 1972. The wines were of very large provenance, however (probably too large), and excellent as they were, they could not reap the benefits of the very best soils. The 1956 was marketed by the Magyar Állami Pincegazdaság, as was the 1972, under the name of Tokaj-Hegyaljai AG Borkombinát.

Grapes infected with *Botrytis cinerea* (the noble rot).

Two other vintages, 1924 and 1931, vinified before World War II, also left an indelible memory. Unfortunately, all the genuine bottles of those years have disappeared due to the events mentioned above. The vineyards were denationalized in 1991, and European capital was plowed into reconstituting the estates each of which once vinified their own wine.

These include the historic, Oremus estate. It is from its vineyards that Tokay Aszü was born. This has nothing to do with the legends which explain the "invention" of Johanisberg dessert wines and Sauternes, which are fairly similar. In the case of Oremus, the story is well-documented. In 1630, Princess Zsuzsanna Lórántffy of Transylvania married György Rákóczy, crown prince of Upper Hungary. Among her vast properties was the Oremus estate, whose wines had the distinction of being labeled *"prima classis."* The family pastor, Szepsi Laczkó Máte, of the University of Wittenberg, introduced the "aszü" vinification

Organoleptic Description

This Tokay Aszü is the result of a traditional blend of 80% Furmint grapes and 20% Harslevelü, but it was vinified in the modern manner. The golden robe shows no signs of oxidation. This is confirmed in the nose by lively apricot aromas which are not too sugary and are faintly spicy. In the mouth, the sugar-acid balance is exemplary. There is elegance, no hint of heaviness and a long finale of very ripe citrus. A beautiful interpretation of an historic wine.

Secrets of quality

Soil type and climate.

Availability

From specialist wine-sellers.

Current price

About FF 200 a half-liter bottle.

Apogee
From 2005 through 2010.

Comparable or almost comparable vintages:
1972 (old style), 1993.

Development:
certainly excellent when thirty years old and almost certainly beyond.

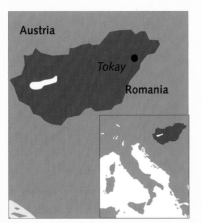

Weather Conditions

In 1995, May was a very sunny month, accelerating the vegetative cycle. The summer was hot and dry. In late September, a few gentle showers hastened the development of *Botrytis cinerea*. October was still sunny and dry, and the nights were particularly chilly. The first snows fell on November 17, while the vines were still green.

method in 1612, and there is proof of production in 1631. The current vineyard was replanted after it was attacked by phylloxera, and more recently, in 1964. To increase the density of plantation and improve the quality of drainage, it was replaced again in 1999 and the first harvest of these new grapes will be in 2003.

In 1995, a large quantity of Aszü were harvested. The 1995 Tokay was made by adding six puttonyos to the basic wine of overripe grapes, meaning that there are six times 150 kilograms of Aszü grapes in six times 136 liters of must. After a ten-hour maceration, the Aszü paste is pressed. The must ferments for two months, then the wine is aged for twenty-six months in small oak barrels from Gönci with a 136-liter capacity. The wine is clarified by being drawn off two or three times, and it continues to mature in half-liter bottles. The syrup measures 11° on the Baumé density scale and contains 67 grams per liter of sugar (expressed as about "11+ 4").

Above:
Tokay Aszü.

Facing page:
A bottle of Tokay Aszü covered in mold.

1. Jacques Chirac
On May 7, Jacques Chirac was elected president of France. The prime minister, Édouard Balladur, another candidate for the presidency from the same political party, resigned.

2. Funeral of Yitzhak Rabin
The funeral of the prime minister of Israel who was assassinated on November 4 by a young Jewish extremist, is held in Jerusalem.

3. Marie-José Pérec
On August 9, this athlete wins France's first gold medal at the World Athletics Championship in Gothenburg, Sweden, running the 400 meters in 49.028 seconds. She is seen here at the Atlanta Olympics in 1996, where she won two gold medals.

4. Terrorist attacks in the Paris Metro
A terrorist explosion at the St.Michel commuter station kills seven and leaves 17 injured.

5. Bibliothèque Nationale de France
France's new National Library was inaugurated on March 30 by President François Mitterrand.

1996

Boris Yeltsin is returned to office in Russia and Bill Clinton in the United States. NASA launches the *Pathfinder* probe of Mars with little publicity. Claudie André-Deshays, the first Frenchwoman in space, completes a sixteen-day flight, fourteen of them on board the *Mir* space station. Jacques Chirac suggests abolishing the draft in France. The United Kingdom in particular and the European Union in general are confronted with the problem of Bovine Spongiform Encephalopathy or BSE ("mad cow disease). Iraq barters petrol for food in a UN agreement. A Boeing 747, flying between New York and Paris, explodes mysteriously over the Atlantic. In Afghanistan, after a two-year siege, the Talibans enter the capital, Kabul, and immediately introduce Moslem *sharia* law. In the United Kingdom, the divorce between the Prince and Princess of Wales becomes final. Belgium is traumatized by the Dutroux affair, a pedophile who has tortured and murdered countless children without being caught. Atlanta hosts the centennial Olympic Games of modern times. France wins the Davis Cup.

Early in the year François Mitterrand dies at the age of 79. Michel Debré, who had been prime minister under General de Gaulle (1959-1962) and one of the founders of the Fifth Republic dies in August. Marguerite Duras, Claude Mauriac, Maria Casarès, Marcello Mastroianni, Ella Fitzgerald, Marcel Carné, and René Lacoste also die that year.

Facing page:
An ancient bottle of Krug Champagne with a stapled cork.

Krug 1996 Champagne

This is not the oldest nor the most powerful brand of champagne but it has immense prestige. The firm was founded in 1843 by Johann-Joseph Krug, who came from Mainz in Germany, and who had learned the art of running a cellar at one of the most prestigious firms of the time, Jacquesson of Châlons. He worked there for six years, married his boss's sister-in-law and went to live in Rheims, where he took over a wine-merchant's. Two years later, he decided to start making his own champagne. He was skilled and his blends were so successful that he was asked to blend the champagnes for other firms. Even today, the Krug vintage champagnes are blended using the techniques established by Johann-Joseph Krug. The formula is 20% Cramant, 20% Vertus-Pierry, 20% Montagne de Reims and 40% Ay-Bouzy.

Johann-Joseph Krug's talents have been inherited by his descendants. Henri Krug—the fifth generation—also excels in blending grapes from a variety of different sources in the Champagne region. Vinification in the traditional way in very small 206-liter casks contributes to the inimitable character of Krug, whose vintages are always awaited with excitement. It is obviously daring to mention a wine which will not be marketed until the end of 2003 at the earliest. But it has been vinified and is now resting in bottles which will eventually put up for sale.

It has been made from rare grapes created in the happiest of conditions because they benefited for sixty-six hours more sunshine than average (4% more).

Organoleptic Description

Here, as an example, are the data for two of the wines from which the Krug Cuvée 1996 has been made:

Verzy : 10.5° (alcohol) – 10.9 g per liter (acidity).

Ay : 11.2° (alcohol) – 10.3 g per liter (acidity).

Only the 1955 and 1928 vintages had such an extreme sugar/acid (alcohol/acid) ratio. A tasting of the "clear wines" from which the champagne is made before it effervesces confirms the analytic data. The wines are as lively as they are powerful and presage a champagne of great character which will age exceptionally well.

Secrets of quality
Contrasting climate, richness and acidity.

Apogee
From 2003
through 2013.

Availability
Not before 2003.

Comparable or almost comparable vintage: 1928.

Current price
None before 2003.

Development:
slow, drink before 2030?

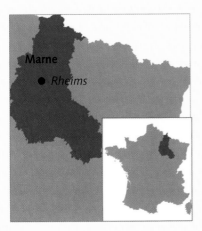

Marne

● Rheims

Weather Conditions

After a normal spring in which there was no frost, flowering began on the first day of the summer solstice. The weather was cool, followed by a long hot spell which lasted from July 10 through August 15. A few showers prevented a drought. The first ten days of September were radiant. The grapes ripened. An unusual chill pervaded the vineyard, and the grapes were harvested in the second week of the month. Rainfall for the season showed a shortfall of 125 ml when compared with the mean. Only the years 1959, 1976, and 1985 were dryer. Another important feature which creates great champagne is the strong contrast between daytime and nighttime temperatures, including very cool nights. This might explain why the grapes of 1996 were very ripe when harvested but had high acidity as well as their content.

Ca' del Bosco Franciacorta 1996 Italian wine

The champagne-makers' representative bodies are excellent and
extremely effective and they mercilessly hound anyone who attempts to
use the magic term "champagne" without having the right to do so.
(There is no question that champagne is the archetypal effervescent
wine, a unique combination of finesse permeated with carbon dioxide.)
At the same time, the term "sparkling wine" has been so greatly abused
that some makers have replaced it with the term "crémant."
Maurizio Zanella became interested in wine-making after visiting the
Romanée-Conti estate. He immediately realised that how important it
was to make a fine wine. Taking Burgundy as a model, he planted a
vineyard with quite a high density of Chardonnay and Pinot Blanc and
Noir varieties in Lombardy.
In 1977, he decided to employ André Dubois, who for a while had been
chief cellarer at Lanson, a champagne-maker, who proved to be of great
help to Ca' del Bosco. A great adventure then began, which lead to the
creation of a sparkling wine applying the champagne method to grapes
from northern Italy.
Maurizio Zanella is an avowed perfectionist. He has his own analytical
laboratory at which data for each wine, at all stages of vinification, are
carefully recorded and compared.
Ca' del Bosco Franciacorta sparkling wine soon became one of the best
Italian wines made by the *"metodo classico"*—which for several years
now, no longer has the right to be called the "méthode champenoise."

Following pages:
in the cellar.

Organoleptic Description

The blend finally adopted consists of 45% Chardonnay, 25% Pinot Blanc and 30% Pinot Noir. The soil is very porous, consisting of a glacial moraine of limestone, sand, and gravel. Vinification is performed in exactly the same way as in Champagne, including long aging on the lees (autolysis of the yeasts), removing the deposit from the neck of the bottle and replacing lost liquid. Never had the clear wines (the still wines before they are made into sparkling wines) attained such a degree of balance and concentration. The 1996 Ca' del Bosco Franciacorta will not go on the market until 2002. The prestige cuvée, Cuvée Anamaria Clementi, is presented in a special bottle. The wine is of great finesse and avoids falling into the trap of heaviness that can affect non-champagne sparkling wines. Vinification was particularly careful. While the wine was still in the process of alcoholic fermentation it was transferred to casks. Malolactic fermentation was followed by aging in wood for six months. When the wine was drawn off into bottles, it was left in cellars at a constant temperature of 12°C (54°F) for five years. This long autolysis of the yeasts adds complexity to a wine already rich in spicy characteristics acquired during aging. This Cuvée of Ca' del Bosco raises it to the first rank of sparkling wines in the world.

Secrets of quality
Cool climate and perfect maturity.

Apogee
From 2003 through 2005.

Availability
From late 2002.

Comparable or almost comparable vintage: 1991.

Current price
Wait until 2002.

Development: preferably to be drunk before 2010.

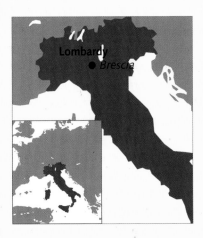

Weather Conditions
In 1996, flowering was uniform and rapid. Two hail storms and a few thunderstorms in the summer made it a cool one, but the grapes were completely ripened and their juice very concentrated.

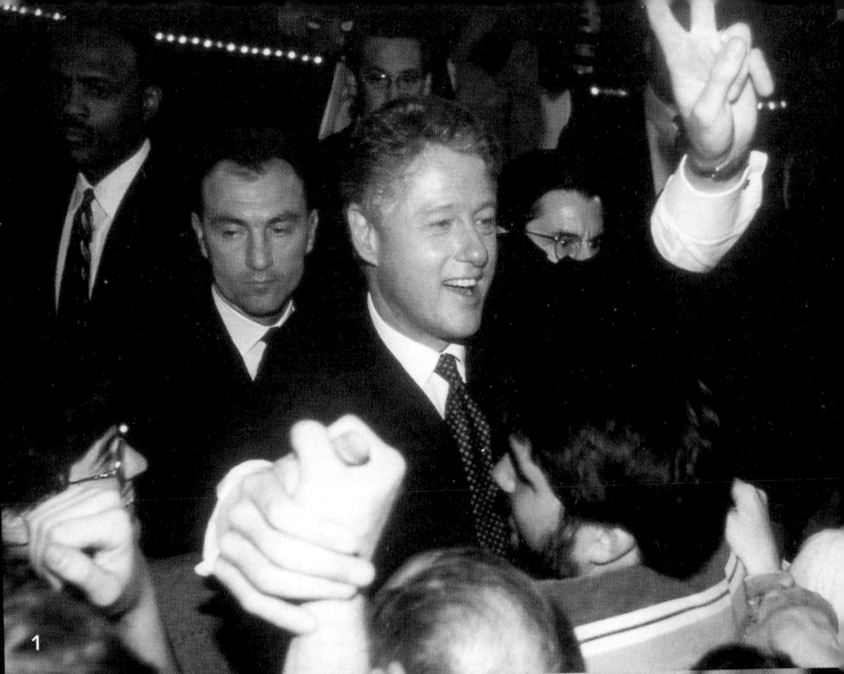

1

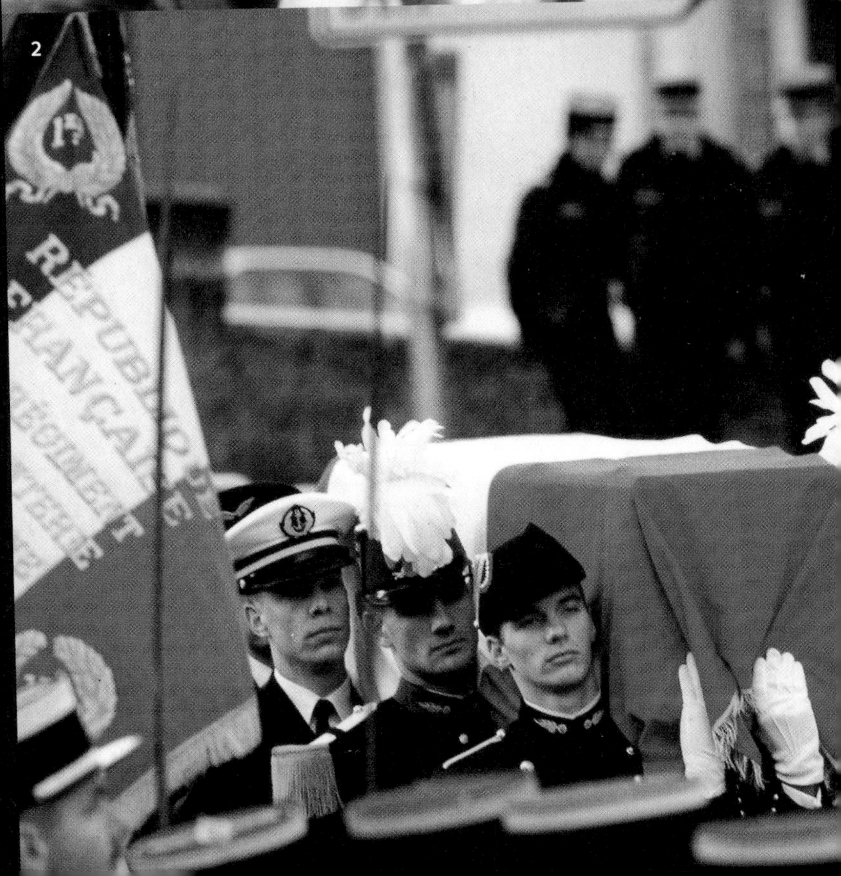

2

1. Bill Clinton
The President of the United States is re-elected for a second four-year term. He is the first Democrat to be re-elected president since Franklin Roosevelt (elected in 1932, 1936, 1940, and 1944).

2. Funeral of François Mitterrand
The former French president died on January 9. The funeral is held at Jarnac (Charentes), while a memorial service is held at Notre-Dame cathedral in Paris.

3. The British Royal Family
The Prince and Princess of Wales divorce.

4. Boris Yeltsin
Investiture of Boris Yeltsin on August 9, in Moscow. The Russian president is re-elected for four years.

5. Marcello Mastroianni
Death of the Italian film star.

Other Great Vintages of the Century

This book cannot be ended without a brief mention of some of the other outstanding wines which have graced the history of the wine-making in the twentieth century.

Two criteria were observed in compiling this list. Mention of a wine-maker already discussed elsewhere in the book has been avoided where at all possible. Similarly, years of great vintages for all French wines, such as 1945 and 1961, have been omitted in order to highlight particularly successful vintages made during less spectacular years.

BORDEAUX

Médoc

• *Margaux*

Château Palmer 1929, 1945, 1961

• *Saint-Julien*

Château Léoville Las Cases 1928, 1929

Château Ducru-Beaucaillou 1921, 1929

Château Beychevelle 1928, 1929

• *Pauillac*

Château Mouton Rothschild 1920

Château Pichon Longueville Comtesse 1918

Château Lynch Bages 1955

• *Saint-Estèphe*

Clos d'Estournel 1926, 1928

Château Montrose 1920, 1921

Château Calon Ségur 1916, 1926

Saint-Émilion

Château Ausone 1906, 1943

Château Canon 1955, 1989

Château Figeac 1906, 1950

Pessac-Léognan

Château Pape Clément 1953, 1959

Domaine de Chevalier 1928, 1953

Pomerol

Château Lafleur 1947

Sauternes

Château Climens 1908, 1937, 1949

Château Coutet, Cuvée Madame 1943, 1949

Château Suduiraut 1959, 1989

Château la Tour Blanche 1921, 1990

Château Gilette, Crème de Tête 1937, 1947

BURGUNDY

Chambertin (producer: Leroy) 1969

Clos de Tart 1985

Echezeaux Jayer 1985

La Tâche 1945, 1953

Corton Clos des Cortons Faiveley 1980

Corton-Charlemagne (producer: Bonneau du Martray) 1985

Corton-Charlemagne (producer: Louis Latour) 1989

Pommard (producer: Hubert de Montille), various climates, 1989

Puligny-Montrachet "Les Pucelles" (Domaine Leflaive) 1978

Chevalier Montrachet (Domaine Leflaive) 1983

Bâtard-Montrachet (producer: Étienne Sauzet) 1989

Montrachet (producers: Comtes Lafon) 1990

ALSACE

Remarkable vintages: 1921 and 1929, 1937, 1945 and 1949, 1953 and 1959, 1971 and 1976, 1983-1985 and 1989, 1990.
Remarkable producers: Zind Humbrecht, Marcel Deiss, Trimbach, Domaine Weinbach (Faller), Boxler, Landmann, Ostertag.

CHAMPAGNE

Rœderer 1949, Cuvée Cristal 1959
Dom Pérignon 1981
Dom Ruinart 1988
Taittinger-Comtes de Champagne 1979, 1985
Krug Clos du Mesnil 1979
Billecart-Salmon, Cuvée NF 1959 and 1961
Pol Roger 1911 and 1921
Charles Heidsieck Royal 1966
De Venoge, Cuvée les Princes, 1976, 1979

PORTUGAL (port wine)

Quinta do Noval 1931
Graham 1935
Warre 1945
Dow 1963
Fonseca 1977
Sandeman 1985
Cockburn 1927

GERMANY

Remarkable vintages: 1911, 1921, 1937, 1945 and 1949, 1953 and 1959, 1971, 1983, 1990.
Remarkable producers: von Schubert (Maximin Grünhäuser Abtsberg), Dr. Tanisch (Bernkasteller Doctor), Schloss Johannisberg, Bürklin-Wolf (Wachenheimer Gerümpel), J. J. Prüm (Sonnenuhr), Langwerth von Simmern (Erbacher Marcobrunn), Staatlichen Weinbaudmänen (Niederhausen-Schlossböckelheim).

ITALY

Remarkable vintages: 1964, 1971, 1978, 1985, 1990.
Remarkable producers:
Piedmont: Ceretto, Aldo Conterno, Bruno Giacosa.
Tuscany: Fratelli Antinori (Tignanello, Solaia, Ornellaia), Col d'Orcia, Tenuta Il Poggione, Villa Banfi.

HUNGARY

Remarkable vintages: 1924, 1931, 1956 and 1972 (two vintages which were unfortunately vinified by the state farm), then 1993 and 1995.
Remarkable producers: Hétszölö, Diskökö, Mégyer, Pajzos, Orémus.

AUSTRIA

Remarkable vintages: 1963, 1981, 1993.
Remarkable producers: Feiler-Artinger, Harald Kraft, Friedrich Seiler, Heidi Schröck.

Glossary

Aging
Between decanting from the fermentation vat and bottling, the wine is placed in another vat or cask where it is allowed to mature. The period, which may last from a few months to several years, is called the aging period.

Alcoholic fermentation
Conversion of the sugar content of the must into alcohol by means of the micro-organisms that cause fermentation.

Ampelography
The science of the vine. One of its aims is to identify grape varieties. An ampelographer is a wine-making expert and historian.

Anthocyanes
Phenolic composite which gives red wine its color.

AOC
Abbreviation for "Appellation d'Origine Contrôlée." French wines made from grapes cultivated within a strictly defined district according to codified methods and vinified according to local custom are granted an AOC.

Assemblage
Blend of wines of the same origin, usually from the same estate but from different grape varieties or different parcels of land. The great wines and the second wine are created by blending.

Ausbruch
Type of Austrian dessert wine.

Auslese

Late harvests. Used in reference to sweet or dry German wines.

Beerenauslese

Type of German dessert wine made from a late harvest, usually affected by noble rot.

Bentonite

Fine powdered clay used for refining wines.

Blanc de blancs

White wine made from white grapes.

Blanc de noirs

White wine made from black (red) grapes.

Botrytis cinerea

Fungal infection responsible for the gray mold so damaging to the quality of the wine but which under certain special conditions, can cause brown, or noble, rot, which is essential for creating the great white dessert wines.

Cap

Name given to solids floating on the surface of the must or wine as it ferments and matures in vats. They consist mainly of skin, seeds, and pulp. The cap is sprayed to extract its color and aromatic content.

Carbonic maceration

Vinification method for grapes that have not been trodden (Beaujolais, for example).

Chaptalisation

Operation consisting of increasing the degree of alcohol in the wine by adding sugar before or during fermentation. Chaptalisation is strictly regulated in France and it is forbidden in wines from the Midi.

Clonal selection

Selection of plants that are genetically identical.

Clone, cutting

Plant obtained by selection for the purpose of asexual propagation.

Collage, clarification

Procedure designed to clarify wines by collecting and discarding the residues in suspension in the bottom of the vat. A colloid (egg white, bentonite, etc.) is added to the wine to encourage precipitation of the deposit.

Crioextraction

Technique for concentrating the juice based on freezing the berries. It is an artificial method of reproducing the effect of frost on the grapes, one which occurs naturally in the German and Canadian vineyards which make Eiswein.

Cuvée

Name given to a particular fine wine. In Champagne, for instance, the word "Cuvée" on the bottle indicates that the wine was made from the first pressing.

Decanting

Transferring wine from a bottle to a carafe, flask, or decanter, in order to leave the lees in the bottle and aerate the wine.

Dropping off, wilt

Failure of grape to form because the flower has not been pollinated or is misshapen, also applied when the immature grapes fall off prematurely. Heavy rain and a cold spell at the wrong time of year are generally to blame for this condition.

Disgorgement

Removal of the deposit that forms in bottles of sparkling wine by extracting it through the mouth.

DOC

Equivalent of the French AOC (q.v.) in Spain, Portugal and Italy (DOCG).

Dosage

Addition of liquor (wine + sugar) to bottles of sparkling wine to top them up after disgorgement. If wine alone is added, the wine is said to be "non-dosed," for which the official description is "brut nature."

Éraflage / égrappage

French term for the practice of separating the twigs and stems of bunches of grapes from the grape berries before fermentation and after the initial treading.

Fermentation vessel

Large wooden, concrete, or stainless steel vessel in which the must is left to ferment. The length of time the must is allowed to ferment and the temperature at which it does so varies according to the wine being made.

Filtration

Pouring the wine through a porous membrane or barrier to strain out the impurities.

Green harvest

Harvesting in summer. Picking the grapes while the leaves are still green tends to reduce the number of usable grapes and consequently the yield per hectare.

INAO

Institut National des Appellations d'Origine Contrôlée. The governing body that regulates the French AOCs.

Lees

Solid matter in suspension in the must or at the bottom of a vat, cask, or hogshead after the wine is drawn off the top. The lees nourish and protect the wine.

Malolactic fermentation

Breaking down the malic acid into lactic acid through the action of lactic bacteria. The wine is made more supple. All red wines are subjected to malolactic fermentation as are white Burgundies, but white Bordeaux wines do not undergo this type of fermentation.

Marc

Solids, mainly grape skins, extracted from the fermentation vat and pressed separately (*See* pressing).

Mass selection

Selection of plants that are genetically different.

Mildew

Fungus disease of vines and other plants. It reached Europe from the United States in the 19th century. To prevent it, vines are treated with Bordeaux mixture (copper sulfate).

Must

Cloudy grape juice prior to fermentation.

Noble rot

See Botrytis cinerea.

Oidium

A wilt caused by a mold of American origin which first appeared on European grapes and other crops in the 19th century. It attacks the leafy parts of the vine and is destroyed by applications of sulfur.

Organoleptic

Pertaining to or perceived by a sensory organ—eyes, nose, and mouth in the case of wine.

Ouillage

French term meaning to top up after a loss of liquid caused by evaporation.

Overripeness

Condition of the grape that is past full maturity. Overripeness is sought after in Bordeaux white dessert wines.

Oxidation

Any substance which fixes oxygen is oxidable, and this is true for most of the components of wine. Aging is caused by oxidation.

Pellicular maceration

Maceration prior to fermentation of grapes that have not been trodden, designed to extract the aromatic elements from the grape skins.

Photosynthesis

The process by which the leaf transforms sunlight into green matter (chlorophyll) and sugar which it then transfers to the grape.

Phylloxera

Plant-louse, accidentally imported from the United States. The insects feed on the roots, causing galls on the leaves and nodules on the roots of the vine. It was first identified in the second half of the 19th century and although it could be partially destroyed by immersing the roots in carbon sulfate, it has never been completely eradicated. The only solution was to graft *Vitis vinifera* onto the roots of American grape varieties, and this saved the French vineyards from complete destruction.

Polyphenols

Phenols (especially anthocyanes and tannins) that are essential constituents of red wines, contributing aroma, color, and structure.

Pressing

Compression of the grape or marc in a press in order to extract the juice. When grapes are pressed, the liquid obtained in a white must. If marc is pressed, a red "pressed wine" is obtained.

Pruning

Cutting back the woody parts of the vine in order to promote fruiting.

Remontage

A French term for a process which consists of taking wine from the bottom of the fermentation vat and sprinkling over the cap and the top of the vat in order to extract the aromatic and phenolic components of the matter floating on the surface. Remontage is performed several times a day for several days running. It also helps to aerate the must.

Residual sugars

Sugars remaining in the wine after alcoholic fermentation.

Root stock

Root on which another vine is grafted. American vine roots are resistant to phylloxera.

Saignée

French term meaning "bleeding." It is the action of removing grape juice from a vat either to produce a rosé wine or to concentrate what remains in the vat.

Sulfuric anhydride (so2)

An aid to vinification which is antioxidant and bacteriocidal. The proportion is regulated as it can constitute a health hazard if used in large quantities.

Soutirage

French term meaning to transfer wine from one vessel to another in order to separate the wine from its lees.

Spätlese

German term meaning "late harvest."

Sulfating

Spraying or dusting vines with a sulfate solution to eliminate fungal pests, such as mildew, oidium, etc. Also used to describe the addition of a sulfurous anhydride to the must or wine to protect it against oxidation and attacks by micro-organisms.

Tannin

A phenolic, astringent, and bitter component, found in the grape-stalks, skins, seeds, and in the wood of the casks, which is an essential ingredient in red wines, especially claret.

Trie

French term used to denote harvesting by picking only those grapes or bunches that are ripe, leaving the rest on the vine. The exercise is performed several times over on the same vines.

Trockenbeerenauslese

Type of German wine resulting from very selective harvesting only of grapes affected by the noble rot.

Variety, stock

Variety of the grapevine cultivated. The European grapevine, *Vitis vinifera,* is divided into about three thousand different varieties which produce vastly differing results when vinified.

Vin de goutte

Red wine produced by pressure of the grapes in the vat.

Vin de presse

Red wine produced by pressing.

Vin marchand

Wine of merchantable or saleable quality. A wine is deemed to be merchantable if it has recognizably good organoleptic qualities when analyzed and tasted.

Vinage

Adding alcohol to a wine. The practice is banned unless it is for the production of a non-sparkling sweet white wine.

Volatil acid

Acid of the acetic type whose content is controlled by regulation (less than a gram per liter which is quite a lot). This is what gives vinegar its flavor.

Addresses of the Winemakers mentioned

FRANCE

Bordeaux

Château Margaux

SC du Château Margaux,

33460 Margaux.

Château Margaux 1900

Château d'Yquem

Comte de Lur-Saluces,

33602 Sauternes.

Château d'Yquem 1921

Château Latour

SCV de Château Latour,

33250 Saint-Lambert.

Château Latour 1928 and 1961

Châteaux Haut-Brion
and La Mission Haut-Brion

SA Domaine Clarence Dillon,

33602 Pessac.

Château Haut-Brion 1989 and

Château la Mission Haut-Brion 1929

Château Mouton Rothschild

Baron Philippe de Rothschild SA

33250 Pauillac.

Château Mouton Rothschild 1945

Château Cheval Blanc

SC du Cheval Blanc,

33330 Saint-Émilion.

Château Cheval Blanc 1947

Château Lafite-Rothschild

SC du Château Lafite-Rothschild,

33250 Pauillac.

Château Lafite-Rothschild 1959

Château Pétrus

SC du Château Pétrus,

33500 Pomerol.

Pétrus 1982

Burgundy

Domaine de la Romanée-Conti

SC du Domaine de la Romanée-Conti,

21700 Vosne-Romanée.

Romanée-Conti 1921

and La Tâche 1937

Domaine du Clos des Lambrays,

21220 Morey-Saint-Denis.

Clos des Lambrays 1945

Domaine Comte Georges de Vogüé

Rue Sainte-Barbe,

21220 Chambolle-Musigny.

Musigny de Vogüé 1949

**Domaine du Château
de Beaune**

Bouchard Père et Fils,

21202 Beaune.

Montrachet 1989

Loire Valley

Château de Fesles

Vignobles Germain and Ass. Loire,

49380 Thouarcé.

Château de Fesles 1947

Rhône Valley

Paul Jaboulet Aîné, les Jalets

La Roche de Glun,

26600 Tain-l'Hermitage.

Hermitage la Chapelle 1961

Château de Beaucastel

Société Fermière Vignobles

Pierre Perrin,

84350 Courthézon.

Château de Beaucastel 1967

Château Rayas

Jacques Reynaud,

84232 Châteauneuf-du-Pape.

Château Rayas 1978

Champagne

Champagne Bollinger

16, rue Jules-Loband ,

51160 Ay.

Bollinger 1911

Champagne Salon

5, rue de la Brèche-d'Oger,

51190 le Mesnil-sur-Oger.

Salon 1928

Champagne Philipponnat

13, rue du Pont,

51160 Mareuil-sur-Ay.

Clos des Goisses 1975

Champagne Moët et Chandon

20, avenue de Champagne,

51200 Épernay.

Dom Pérignon 1985

**Champagne
Veuve Clicquot Ponsardin**

12, rue du Temple,

51100 Rheims.

Veuve Clicquot Grande Dame 1990

Champagne Krug

5, rue Coquebert,

51100 Rheims.

Krug 1996

GERMANY

Weingut Egon Müller

D-54459 Wiltingen, Scharzhof.

Scharzhofberger Auslese 1971

**Domänenweingut
Schloss Schönborn**

Hauptstrasse 53,

D-65347 Hattenheim, Rheingau.

Hattenheimer Pfaffenberg 1976

AUSTRALIA

Read MacCarthy Group

604-606 Harris St.

Ultimo, NSW 2007

Penfolds Grange 1962

AUSTRIA

**Weingut Elisabeth
und Friedrich Seiler**

Setzgasse, 10, 7071 Rust.

Ruster Ausbruch 1934

SPAIN

Bodega Vega Sicilia SA

Valbuena de Duero,

47359 Valladolid.

Vega Sicilia 1970

Bodega Alejandro Fernandez

Real, 2. Pesquera de Duero,

47359 Valladolid.

Pesquera Janus Reserva 1982

UNITED STATES

Diamond Creek Vineyards

1500 Diamond Mountain Road

Calistoga, CA 94515.

Diamond Creek Lake 1994

HUNGARY

Oremus

András Bacsó, Bajcsy-zs u. 45,

3934 Tolcsva.

Tokay Aszü 1995

ITALY

Franco Biondi Santi

Tenuta Greppo, Loc Greppo, 183

53024 Montalcino.

Brunello di Montalcino 1964

Tenuta San Guido

Marchesi Nicolo incisa

della Rocchetta

57020 Bolgheri.

Sassicaia 1985

Gaja Società Semplice

Azienda Agricola,

via Torino n. 36/a

12050 Barbaresco.

Barbaresco Sori San Lorenzo 1989

Azienda Agricola
Ca' del Bosco SPA

Via Case Sparse, 20,

25030 Erbusco.

Ca' del Bosco 1996

PORTUGAL

Taylor Fladgate & Yeatman

Rua do Choupelo, 250,

4400-088 Vila Nova de Gaia.

Taylor port, 1935

Photographic credits

Agencies

KEYSTONE – pages 102-103 (except photo 3), 112-113 (except photo 5), 124-125 (except photo 5), 136-137 (except photo 3), 143 (except photo 3), 151 (except photo 3), 156-157 (except photo 3), 162-163 (except photos 2 and 5), 174-175 (except photos 1 and 5), 186-187 (except photo 1), 196-197 (except photos 1 and 5), 202-203 (except photos 1 and 4), 225, 233 (except photo 4), 238-239 (except photos 2 and 5), 246 photo 1, 254-255 (except photos 3 and 5), 272 photo 2.

SYGMA – pages 280-281, 290-291, 306-307, 324-325 (photo 1: 1999 Johann Otto Von Spreckelsen), 334-335, 342-343, 352-353, 362-363.

KEYSTONE-SYGMA – pages 103 photo 3, 125 photo 5, 137 photo 3, 142-143 (except photos 4 and 5), 150-151 (except photos 3 and 4), 156 photo 3, 162 photo 2, 163 photo 5, 174 photo 1, 175 photo 5, 186 photo 1, 196 photo 1, 197 photo 5, 202 photo 1, 203 photo 4, 214-215, 224, 232-233 (except photos 3 and 5), 238 photo 2, 239 photo 5, 246-247 (except photo 1), 255 (except photo 4), 264-265, 272-273 (except photo 2).

MAGNUM – page 47.

SCOPE
Archives of the Bordeaux Chamber of Commerce, page 41.
Jean-Luc Barde, pages 39, 43, 58, 65, 73, 79, 80-81, 87, 88-89, 191, 223.
Isabelle Eshraghi, page 34.
Daniel Gorgeon, page 26 (bottom).
Philip Gould, page 340.
Jacques Guillard, pages 13, 17 (top and bottom), 19, 20, 21, 26 (top and middle), 35 (middle), 38, 57, 63, 69, 75, 76, 77, 117, 145, 159, 171, 172, 241, 249, 250 and 253, 251, 252, 267, 275, 287, 345, 347, 350, 351, 355.
Michel Guillard, pages 14, 16, 23, 27, 30-31, 99, 295.
Frédéric Hadengue, page 17 (middle).
Francis Jalain, pages 12, 35 (bottom).
Kaktus, pages 84-85.
Sara Matthews pages 11, 83.
Michel Plassart, page 15.
Nick Servian, pages 91, 92-93.

French producers

Baron Philippe de Rothschild SA, pages 166 and 167, 168-169 (archives).
Champagne Bollinger, pages 24 (archives), 105 (archives), 106 and 111, 107, 110 (archives).
Champagne Krug, pages 356 and 357.
Champagne Moët et Chandon, pages 293, 294 and 299, 298.
Champagne Philipponnat, pages 258 and 261, 259, 260, 262, 263.

Champagne Salon, pages 132-135, 133 (archives), 134 (archives).

Champagne Veuve Clicquot Ponsardin, pages 45, 257, 327, 328-333, 329, 330-331, 332.

Château d'Yquem, pages 49 (archives).

Domaine du Château de Beaune, pages 318- 321, 319, 320.

Domaine du Clos des Lambrays, pages 170 and 173 (Jean-Louis Bernuy).

Domaine Comte Georges de Vogüé, pages 192 and 193, 194-195 (archives).

Domaines Perrin, pages 235, 236 and 237.

Paul Jaboulet Aîné, pages 205, 206 and 207, 208-209 (archives).

SA du Domaine Clarence Dillon (photographs by Burdin), pages 140-141, 310-313, 311, 312.

SC du Château Margaux, pages 97 (archives), 100 (archives), 98-101.

SC du Château Lafite-Rothschild, pages 199, 200-201.

SC du Cheval Blanc, pages 178 and 181, 180 (archives).

SC du Domaine de la Romanée-Conti, pages 118, 160 and 161.

SCV de Château Latour, pages 29 (archives), 35 (archives), 127 (archives), 128-129, 209-213.

Vignobles Germain et Associés Loire, pages 25, 184-185.

Foreign Producers

Bodega Alejandro Fernandez, pages 286-289, 288.

Bodega Vega Sicilia SA, pages 242-245, 243, 244.

Diamond Creek Vineyards, page 339.

Domänenweingut Schloss Schönborn, pages 268- 269, 270-271.

Franco Biondi Santi (Tenuta Greppo), pages 66-67, 227, 228- 231, 229, 230.

Gaja Società Semplice, page 316.

Marchesi Incisa della Rocchetta (Tenuta San Guido), pages 300-303, 301, 302.

Orémus, pages 346-349, 348.

Read MacCarthy Group, pages 218-221, 219, 220.

Taylor Fladgate & Yeatman, pages 153 (archives), 154-155.

Weingut Elisabeth und Friedrich Seiler, pages 146-149, 147, 148.

As well as

Archives Départementales de la Côte-d'Or, page 9.

Michel Blanc/Comité de Promotion de Châteauneuf-du-Pape, page 278.

Christie's Wine Department pages 33, 115, 116 and 119, 120–123, 139, 165, 167, 177, 189, 201, 213, 217, 222, 276, 277 and 279, 283, 284- 285, 304-305, 309, 315, 322, 323, 337.

CIVC (Comité Interprofessionnel du Vin de Champagne) Collection, pages 54-55 (Visuel Impact), 296-297 (Jean-Paul Paireault), 360-361 (Rohrscheid).

Laziz Hamani/Éditions Assouline, pages 28, 36, 37, 50-51, 130-131, 211, 212, 314-317, 338- 341, 358-359.

Mme de Labarre, pages 182-183.

Denis Mollat, page 179.

Jean-Pierre Procureur, pages 108-109, 113 (photo 5).

City of Rust, pages 60-61.

Contents

The author and the publisher would particularly like to thank:
Monsieur Philippe Pascal, whose idea it was to produce this book, Mr Thomas
Hudson (Christie's), Filippa Tiago (Maison Veuve Clicquot Ponsardin), Madame
de Labarre, Monsieur Denis Mollat, Monsieur Jean-Pierre Procureur, Madame
Marika Nacajo, Monsieur Andras Bacso, Madame Jeannine Coureau, the CIVC
(Comité Interprofessionnel du Vin de Champagne), Monsieur Michel Blanc
(Fédération des Syndicats de Producteurs de Châteauneuf-du-Pape), and Bernard
Ginestet, as well as all the producers who contributed illustrations for this work.
Our thanks also to the Scope, Sygma, and Keystone photographic agencies who did
so much to make this book a success.